REVELATIONS ON THE ROAD

a pilgrim journey

Lynn W. Huber

Copyright © 2003 by Lynn W. Huber
All Rights Reserved.
No part of this book may be reproduced or transmitted in any form or
by any means, graphic, electronic, or mechanical, including photocopying,
recording, taping or by any information storage or retrieval system,
without the permission in writing from the publisher.
Published by WovenWord Press
811 Mapleton Ave.
Boulder, CO 80304
www.wovenword.com

Cover photo © 2003 by Sheila Durkin Dierks
Cover and book design © 2003 by Vicki McVey
Photographs © 2003 by Frank A. Huber

ISBN: 0 9719383 4 2
PCN: 20031131911

DEDICATION

To Frank:
My dear companion on the journey,
my greatest fan and
my most constructive critic.

CONTENTS

Acknowledgments	v
Foreword	vi
Introduction	ix

Part 1: Discoveries About The Spiritual Journey — 1

Revelation 1:	It Is God Seeking Us	3
Revelation 2:	Faith is Mostly About Trust	9
Revelation 3:	Conversion Is Putting God in the Center	17

Part 2: Struggles and Signposts From My Life on the Road — 27

Revelation 4:	Being A Woman Matters	29
Revelation 5:	Dealing with the *Why?* Question	41
Revelation 6:	It's All of Us or None	51
Revelation 7:	On Aging as a Spiritual Journey	61

Part 3: The Mystery of Prayer — 75

Revelation 8:	The Gift of Prayer	77
Revelation 9:	Teach Me What I Need to Know	89
Revelation 10:	Be Here Now (Time As A Spiritual Issue)	99

Part 4: You Cannot Go it Alone — 119

Revelation 11:	Community, Friendship, Marriage and the Body of Christ	121

Epilogue	147
Notes	151
References	153

ACKNOWLEDGMENTS

This project has had many midwives, some of whom appear in its pages, and most of whom cannot be formally acknowledged. I would give specific note of several who can, however.

First is Richard Morgan, who first suggested that I commit some of my teaching stories to paper. I thank you, Richard, for that, as well as for your generous forward to this book.

Jane Thibault has inspired me for a long time, and her encouragement kept me on the path in this endeavor. For this I thank you, Jane.

John Mogabgab read my manuscript early on and encouraged me to seek a publisher; trusting his judgment and benefiting from his support, I did. Thank you, John.

Finding WovenWord Press was a serendipitous gift of God. Sheila Dierks, publisher, not only provided encouragement, wise counsel and love, but gifted me with the cover photo for this book, which would not have been born without her. Thank you, Sheila.

Vicki McVey, my editor, used skill, tact, love and wisdom in helping to bring this book to birth—whole and healthy. Vicki, I offer you hearty thanks.

Words can only hint at how much I thank my beloved husband, Frank, for so many gifts offered during the long process during which this book was gestating. His constant patience, the gifts of meals cooked and time together surrendered, the words read over and over, all are deeply appreciated. When the time came for decisions about how the book would look, Frank's offer of his photos for the inner pages of the book (not to mention hours of helping me select them) make this a truly joint venture. Thank you, Frank, beyond what words can say.

Finally I thank you, valued reader and fellow pilgrim. I have often prayed during the writing and editing of this book that God would work through it to bless you. It is for you that it was written. May your own path take you to wholeness, joy and fruitfulness in discovering your own revelations on the road.

Lynn W. Huber
November 2003

FOREWORD

Our situation today is like *The Rhyme of the Ancient Mariner,* "Water, water everywhere, nor any drop to drink." We live in a vast ocean of books about spirituality. Yet we still lack a spirituality that connects God's story and our own life story. Like the Ancient Mariner, who will die unless he escapes drinking salt water from the sea, so we too need to find a source of pure water if we are not to die of spiritual thirst.

What captivates me about Lynn Huber's *Revelations on the Road* is the way she connects her story with scripture and the work of the Spirit in her life. As she tells her story—how the Spirit speaks to her through what seem meaningless, insignificant events—her story moves and inspires us. In so doing she blazes a trail for all who seek to journal God's nudges in their own stories.

Her book is full of varied experiences, both in graced moments, and with significant people who touched her life. We hear about Clair and Rabbi Falk, and Mr. Pompiani, Roberta and Fr. John Hugo, and many others. Lynn chronicles her own spiritual journey, first as a Jew in a Christian society, and then as a Christian, raised as a Jew.

Dr. Huber tells about her pilgrimage of faith, and her experiences of marginality as a Jew, a Christian, a woman teaching in an all-male environment, a layperson amidst a clergy-dominated church system, and a liberal. Since she had known the pain of being an outcast, she can connect with others on the boundaries of life.

Her book consists of eleven revelations that come to her on her pilgrimage. She deals honesty with faith issues, such as "original sin," "the feminine face of God," and the big *why* question. Of particular interest is her chapter on "Aging as a Spiritual Journey," in which she declares that "when you work with older adults, you work on your own spiritual journey." That has been my conviction and passion for the past twenty five years! So I resonate with much in this book.

The book ends with three revelations about the mystery of prayer, and the meaning of community and marriage. Through these pages Lynn sees the goal of the spiritual journey as "Live all our lives in the House of God." She well reaches that goal in her own life, and points the way for others, too.

Of special import are the exercises at the end of each chapter. We journey alone, but we need companions along the way. Here Lynn provides skillful practices which would help any group to experience its own revelations on the road. One will also find a wealth of resources for additional reading in this book.

CLOSING THOUGHTS

The woman at the well came for water from a well. After meeting Jesus she left with "living water, which became in her a spring of water gushing up to eternal life." That is the fervent hope and desperate need of everyone in this spiritual wasteland.

Lynn Huber has been generous in sharing her story at numerous conferences and retreats across this nation. Now, at last, we have in print her gems of experience as we work on our own journeys and with others. When you read this book, you will be moved and stirred to find how God has been at work in your life. What more can any of us ask?

Richard L. Morgan, Ph.D.
Author, Presbyterian Minister and Leader of Spiritual Autobiography Groups.
North Huntingdon, Pa.

Introduction
The Birth of This Book

St. Paul had a revelation on the road to Damascus. It temporarily blinded him, knocked him off his course, utterly changed his self-image, and irrevocably transformed his understanding of the purpose of his life (see the story in Acts 9 and Acts 22).

My journey has not been marked by such a singular, life-changing revelation. Sometimes I am embarrassed by the way in which my life has gone, for it seems that it is in tiny, almost unnoticeable happenings that my greatest learnings have come. There is a Biblical parable for this. Jesus tells of the mustard seed (Mt 13:31), the tiny unnoticeable seed out of which God can grow towering mustard trees.

Elijah also discovered the power of the small. When he escaped into the desert to avoid the wrath of Jezebel, he encountered God. The Bible recounts a strange series of natural wonders that occurred while Elijah hid in a cave, but assures us that it was not in these dramatic events that Elijah found God. Although first there was a wind that tore the very rocks and mountains apart, then an earthquake, then a fire, the text says that God was not in the wind, the earthquake or the fire (I Kgs 19:11 ff). Instead God came in what is variously translated as "a still small voice," "a gentle whisper," and "a sound of sheer silence." For Elijah too, God comes in the little, the quiet, the almost unnoticeable.

In my work as a teacher, retreat leader, and spiritual director I have found others encouraging me to share the stories of my mustard seeds, which I now call my *revelations on the road*. I believe that these fragments of my story are not mine to hoard but are there to be passed on. This belief has evolved from promptings that come either directly during prayer or indirectly from other people. I am grateful for all these promptings.

I believe in the importance of story and story sharing. The belief is so strong that I call it my credo, and include it in my professional brochure:

My Credo

I believe that the greatest gift we can offer to each other is the telling of and listening to our stories. This empowers us to appropriate and to live out our own stories, unifies us in diversity, and leads to reconciliation.

This theme of story unifies all I do: including work with older adults (who have a developmental as well as a spiritual need to recover and share their stories); evangelism (the sharing of how my story, your story and "the story" connect); spiritual direction (an intimate vehicle for exploring and living into one's story); lay pastoral care training (helping people learn how to elicit and validate others' stories); retreat work (an opportunity to gather with others to explore our stories), and work with congregations and judicatory bodies (which have their own stories).

I also believe in community: the people God has provided to accompany us for a time on our journeys. My community consists not only of those I see and talk to in person, but those whose lives I have been blessed to touch through biography, through prayer (in the Communion of Saints), and through their writings.

Shortly before beginning this book I spent almost six weeks in a very restful space—required (and permitted) by my need to recover from a bout with pneumonia. During that time I experienced the community of writers in a powerful way, finding one introducing me to another, that one to yet another. Even the themes they addressed seemed to interconnect in powerful ways. Two of the authors were contemporary women who had written personal, spiritual journey books that mined their own life experience and offered the discovered (and refined) ore to others, including me.

My first activity after the illness was to participate in a conference at which the author of one of those books, Jane Thibault, was also present. Her book (1993) had also gestated for a long time, and had been given birth only after a rest enforced by an injury. Jane encouraged me to write this book, and I am grateful to her. Another presenter at the same conference was Richard Morgan, who, two years before, had come up to me and said, "Lynn, you should be writing. I've just had a book published, and if you decide you want to do this, I'll try to help you." So I felt supported by and welcomed into the community of contemporary spiritual writers.

Some time after I was well into the writing I began to feel very vulnerable. I feared that I might be engaged in a narcissistic exercise of interest to myself alone, and questioned whether it really was a ministry to others. I was also aware of having written things that I know in my head to be true, but which I knew I had not yet fully learned to live out in practice, and I wondered if I had the right to share them.

Then, upon the rare and strong insistence of my spiritual director, I read Jean Shinoda Bolen's *Crossing to Avalon.* Bolen ends the book with a comment about story-sharing, which came as a gift to me, in part because of her use of the word "revelations."

> _To bring about a paradigm shift in the culture that will change assumptions and attitudes, a critical number of us have to tell the stories of our personal revelations and transformations_ (emphasis included). . . . _The stories people tell have a way of taking care of them. If stories come to you, care for them. And learn to give them away where they are needed. Sometimes a person needs a story more than food to stay alive_ (pp. 272-273).

Synchronicity, the apparently accidental coming together of things that have meaning, is something that I believe is often not accidental at all. (More about this later.) Your reading this book at this time is no accident. My going to that conference right after recovering from pneumonia was no accident. One of my favorite sayings is, "A coincidence is a miracle in which God wishes to remain anonymous." So, prompted by these many urgings and nudgings, I offer you some gleanings from my life, in hopes that you may intentionally join this community of pilgrims and thereby find yourself affirmed and challenged.

YOUR PILGRIM JOURNEY WITH THIS BOOK

This book is designed to be lived with, rather than just read, although you may use it any way that works for you. Each chapter is titled for a _revelation_, an insight that has come, sometimes rapidly and sometimes gradually. Sometimes it has come with a flash of humor and great delight, and sometimes in the midst of pain, fear and confusion.

The genesis of each insight in my life experience is described, so you can get a sense of its lived reality. Implications of the insight are explored, and the ways in which others (including the writers of scripture) have dealt with the issues involved are sometimes included. You are invited to see where you might have learned, or be called to learn, the application of each revelation to your own life.

Exercises are provided so that you can work with your own material, pray with it, journal about it, and come to comprehend it more fully. These exercises are collected in a section at the end of each chapter entitled "Making the Story Your Own." Luke (2:19) tells us that Mary of Nazareth *pondered* events in her life. I love the word *ponder*. And I invite you to ponder the events in your own life. For all the stories in the story of God are part of one larger story. We cannot truly know this until we weave our own story into The Story, and thus come in joyful wonder to discover our common seeking, our common finding, our common road.

Do not feel that you have to do all of the exercises at once. Choose those which speak to you, and give yourself permission to come back later to some of the other ones if you wish. In this, as in all things, be gentle with yourself.

A book which has touched me deeply is *The Sacred Dimensions of Women's Experience,* edited by Elizabeth Dodson Gray. She says (p.1) that women do theology differently from the abstract way men traditionally have done it. Women do it "in the particular;" their writings are "clothed in the subjective." She confirms my sense that God speaks to us in the particularities of our own lives, in a language somehow mysteriously unique for each person.

My prayer for you is that God will allow you to connect your story with mine and with those of others we explore together, and that in the connection your own pilgrimage will be enriched.

PART 1:
Discoveries About the Spiritual Journey

Discoveries About the Spiritual Journey

Revelation One: It is God Seeking Us

As a little girl I was hungry and restless. I hungered for knowledge, and asked an endless stream of *why* questions that drove my mother nuts. I hungered for certainty. So, for example, I opened all of the little wrappers containing my father's razor blades, to be sure that each held its proper contents. I hungered for connections with people, and indiscriminately climbed into the laps of those who came to visit in our home. There was an insatiability about these hungers; it might be expressed as the never-ending need for "something more."

Sometimes when I was feeling especially hungry, lonely, fearful, or angry, that Something drove me out of the house and up to the top of a hill that concealed a nearby reservoir. The reservoir was a gift because it served as a buffer against the encroaching city, preserving a peaceful, open, green space with a small number of trees and even fewer people. Up on that hill, alone, that Something somehow touched my heart and, at least for those moments, stilled the hunger. At the time I did not call those experiences prayer, but that's what they were.

Several decades later I read Abraham Heschel's magnificent book *God in Search of Man*. Heschel articulated for me the notion that God was even more hungry for me than I for God, and that God was actively and always searching me out.

> *Revelation means that the thick silence which fills the endless distance between God and the human mind was pierced, and (humanity)[1] was told that God is concerned with the affairs of (humankind); that not only does (humanity) need God, God is also in need of (humankind). It is such knowledge that makes the soul of Israel immune to despair.*

Such knowledge immunizes my soul too.

Furthermore, Heschel makes a distinction between the mystic, one in search of God, and the prophet, one whom God seeks out:

> *Unlike the mystic act, revelation is not the result of a quest for esoteric experience. What characterizes the prophet is, on the contrary, an effort to escape such experience. Never does s/he relish (a) vision as one relishes the attainment of a goal longed for. Revelation is not an act of . . . seeking, but of . . . being sought after, an act in God's search of humanity.*

I believe that we are *all* both mystic and prophet. At times we seek God in the darkness, and experience God as coy lover. At other times we flee God who appears as the hunter. And sometimes in our confusion, hope and fear, God seems like both lover and hunter at once.

Francis Thompson (1986) spent many years running from and being pursued by God, a journey he recorded powerfully in his poem "The Hound of Heaven," from which the following short excerpt is taken:

> *I fled Him, down the nights and down the days;*
> *I fled Him, down the arches of the years;*

I fled Him, down the labyrinthine ways
Of my own mind . . .
I hid from Him . . .
From those strong Feet that . . .followed after . . .
A Voice beat
More instant than the Feet—
"All things betray thee, who betrayest Me."

I have my own labyrinthine ways. The process of rereading my journals brought back many hitherto forgotten memories of God's searching and my hiding. With some shock I found repeated evidence of having been taught difficult lessons and then promptly having forgotten them, later recording in the journal other incidents that taught me the same lessons, as though I had never come across them before.

It was as if God were a dog trainer and I a puppy. A lesson is taught many times before it sticks, but the patient trainer just keeps on teaching, trusting that finally the lesson will embed itself in permanent pathways in the puppy's mind and heart. The evidence of God's patient, persistent, even relentless pursuit of me was humbling, encouraging and awe-inspiring at one and the same time.

It seems that some of these lessons can only be learned through the retrospective lens. We do not get it the first time, and the reinforcements are only effective because they are repeated and then reflected upon. Soren Kierkegaarde said, "Life is lived forward but understood backward" (Missine, 1990:18). Perhaps the most powerful of the lessons we learn while looking backward is how the hound of heaven has been on our trail.

While the personal assurance that God seeks us comes in part as a result of our own encounters with God, we can also learn from similar experiences of others. The scriptural assurance that God seeks us out is vast. It ranges from the stories of God's calls to Abraham and Sarah, Moses, Joseph, Gideon, Deborah (in fact all of the prophets), to Jesus, and all of the disciples, to some wonderful general reassurances in the Gospels and Epistles[2]. Listen to just a tiny sampling.

Listen:

I will now allure her (Israel), and bring her into the wilderness, and speak tenderly to her (Hos 2:14).

Listen:

How often have I desired to gather your children together as a hen gathers her brood under her wings, and you were not willing! (Mt 23:37)

Listen:

For God so loved the world that God sent God's only begotten child so that all who believe in him should have everlasting life (Jn 3:16).

Listen:

Draw near to God and God will draw near to you (Jas 4:8).

Listen:

Listen! I am standing at the door, knocking; if you hear my voice and open the door I will come in to you and eat with you and you with me (Rv 3:20).

God *is* ever more ready to seek us out than we are to engage with God. Knowing this is paradoxically both a comfort and a threat. For to engage with God is always to know one's own tininess; to engage with God is always to be on the verge of yet another surrender; to engage with God means in one mysterious way or another selling all we have and giving to the poor; to engage with God means standing on the edge of a precipice and being willing to jump, if called.

Why do it? Because, as Francis Thompson (1986) says, "All things betray thee, who betrayest me." When Peter and the disciples watched many followers of Jesus leaving because Jesus' words were too hard, Jesus turned to them and said, "Do you also wish to go away?" Peter responded, "Lord, to whom can we go? You have the words of eternal life"(Jn 6:67-68). So I keep on. And I encourage you to keep on too, because without God all things betray. Without God there is truly nowhere to go.

MAKING THE STORY YOUR OWN

◆ In your own life, where have you been conscious (at the time or in retrospect) of God pursuing you? How did you flee? What were the fears that propelled you to avoid the encounter?

◆ Try writing a dialogue with Jesus in which he starts by saying to you: "Listen! I am standing at the door, knocking; if you hear my voice and open the door I will come in to you and eat with you and you with me" (Rv 3:20). How do you respond? Write your response, his answer, and yours to him, etc. until the dialogue feels finished for you. Then ponder it in your heart.

◆ Think of a time when you had a task that seemed too big for you, but which you were convinced was what you were meant (called) to do. What threatened to distract you from the path (fear, busy-ness, a sense of your own importance)? What happened? How do you now see God as having worked through this experience in your life?

◆ What stories in scripture or elsewhere about fleeing God have touched you? Spend some time with one or more of them, putting yourself into the place of the character(s) with whom you most close-ly identify. What lessons do you learn? What principles can you take from this to be guideposts on your future way? (If you find this choice difficult, consider being Gideon. Read his story in Judges (6:11 ff.) and imagine it is your story. Or get the video *It's a Wonderful Life* and imagine yourself in the role of the main character.)

Revelations on the Road

FOR FURTHER READING

Heschel, Abraham Joseph. 1997. *God in Search of Man: A Philosophy of Judaism.* New York: Noonday Press.

Thompson, Francis. 1986. *The Hound of Heaven.* New York: Morehouse Press.

Revelation Two: "Faith Is Mostly About Trust"

Background and Initial Conversion

My family was nominally Jewish. My mother had been raised in New York City as a member of the Ethical Cultural Society, a late nineteenth century offshoot of Reform Judaism. It had no creed or theology, but worked to enhance the ethical sensitivity of its members, and stressed both intellectual rigor and social responsibility. My father's family was affiliated with a Reform Jewish temple in Richmond, Virginia.

When I was little we celebrated Christmas—and it was a joyous cele-
bration. I remember it as being filled with fun, surprise and mystery. When I
was about seven I began attending the religious school at Temple and
learning about Jewish stories and holidays. I asked my folks why, if we were
Jewish, we ignored them. We began to celebrate Chanukah instead of
Christmas, and to light candles on the Sabbath. I became proud of Jewish
traditions, and particularly of the heritage of intellectual excellence and
ethical responsibility.

While I was a first year college student, I was invited by my home Rabbi
to give a sermon. In it I said that I sensed I was using the word *God* dishon-
estly to mean two entirely separate and unrelated things, neither of which
alone was what I felt God should be.

One was, the God of the deist, the Prime Mover, the creator of the universe, the One who developed Natural Law—so that corn makes corn and
people make people and two and two make four and the planets stay in
orbit. But while I was grateful for the order and predictability of the universe,
the Prime Mover was totally impersonal, uninvolved in the daily workings of
the world, and totally unsatisfactory to me. While I was not able at the time
to articulate it, or, if able, unwilling to accept the neediness involved, I was
seeking a *relationship* with whatever God was.

The second meaning was something which I felt to be present within
humankind. It might equally well be called love or truth or beauty or spirit.
This spirit, however, had no connection that I could see to the Prime Mover,
and this concept was equally unsatisfying. I ended the sermon with the
words, "Perhaps only the search is God." The coming together of these two
notions of God occurred for me when I became a full fledged Trinitarian
Christian. Up until that time I had dismissed Christianity out of hand, viewing
all Christians as morally and intellectually inferior. I believed that they were
morally inferior because of the Holocaust (and I still believe Christianity as a
whole bears a terrible responsibility for that horror). I believed that they were
intellectually inferior because when they got to be seven and learned there
was no Santa Claus, they didn't have the moral courage to stand alone. So
they made Santa younger, and called him Jesus. I didn't know *what* God

was, but whatever God was, I was sure God was *not* a young and hand-some Santa Claus with a light brown beard!

If you have read Paul's sermon to the Athenians (Acts 17: 22 ff), you know that Paul taught by starting with his listeners' own life experience. He began by looking at the Athenians' altar "to an unknown God," and tying that in with the God who "made the world and everything in it," and in whom "we live and move and have our being" (vv. 23, 24, 28). His audience was thus able to hear him.

In college I fell in love with a man who was a Christian, now an old and dear friend, who played Paul for me. He began with my experience, and told me of a God whose name Orthodox Jews are not even permitted to pronounce, for to say "The Name" is to limit the illimitable. He acknowl-edged that this is a God whom I could not comprehend; yet a God who did make the world. He argued however that God is not an absent or disin-terested party, that God does indeed care about humankind (though we do not know why), and that God has chosen to let us know this by taking on the human condition and living it with us. God has chosen to be caught in the crunch of time and space and fragile flesh, has chosen to live in the agony of finite knowledge and perspective, has chosen to become in-car-nate (that is, in the flesh) in order to say to me and to all of us, "I love you."

Somehow I heard it! In fact, I became a Christian because of the incar-nation, not because of the crucifixion. And even at this point in my life it still seems to me to be a much more "crucifying" thing for God to have entered our world, than to have left it, in no matter how cruel a fashion. I have been told by some Christian friends that it takes a Jew to understand the incarnation. Whether this is true or not, my awareness of the sanctity of L'Chaim—life—is interpenetrated with my awareness that Creator God has also chosen to live it as we do. And for me the third part of the Trinity, the Spirit, is understood in one way as another manifestation of incarnation, of our being made in the image of God, with Spirit here and now—in Whom we live and move and have our being.

The word for spirit in many languages—*pneuma* (Greek), *spiritus* (Latin) and *Ruach* (Hebrew) among them—also means breath, air, and wind. This is also true in Sanskrit and Lakota. The fact that such different cultures tie these concepts together says something important to me. We are surrounded by, filled with, move through, and *have our being* literally in SPIRIT—in air, breath, wind. And this is something that is intuitively grasped as truth, regardless of the words and culture of the people who experience it.

THE FEARS

While all of this was wonderful, for a long time I retained a little Ethical Culture/Jewish lady who sat on my shoulder and periodically whispered in my ear, "You know this is crazy-making, don't you?" She frightened me; I had times of great fear.

From the beginning I have known enough about psychology to know that if one makes a real commitment to something, it transforms everything else in one's personality and in one's life. That is scary. I spoke to myself: "What if I believe, and the belief is false? Perhaps worse, what if it is true, and I make commitments to God, and God makes *demands* on me? What might they be? I have been carefully taught not to sign blank checks, yet it sometimes feels like that is what I am being asked to do."

And that is *exactly* what we are being asked to do. It is only possible to say "yes" if we have such trust in God that we know that writing the check will always be in our own best interest, no matter how costly it seems.

I have had times of unnamable fear. I love some of Gerard Manley Hopkins' fierce, dark poems that seem to express my own experience. One ends with the words "Wrestling with, Oh my God, my God!." I understand this in my deepest being, for I identify with Jacob—who wrestled with the angel, got his hip put out of joint, and received a new identity and a new name. Most of the time I like my old body, identity and name pretty well, thank you, and don't want them changed.

Early on perhaps I was most of all afraid that there would be a conflict between reason and faith, and I knew that I would have to be true to what seemed reasonable to me if I were to maintain any personal integrity. I found myself at three o'clock one morning sitting on the floor of our house in a narrow hall between the stairs and a second story bedroom. Behind me was a wall, against which I leaned; In front of me was a wrought iron railing. I felt, both literally and figuratively, as if I were in jail. For I knew that if I made one more step on this road that I could not turn back, and I did not know where it was taking me. I profoundly feared a total loss of control. Even more, I feared for my very being—because I trusted my mind above any part of me, and my mind did not understand what was going on. I knew that I did not accept the Creed, at least as I understood it, yet that was what the church seemed to be founded on, and increasingly I knew that I *must* be in the church. There seemed no viable way out, and I was utterly miserable.

Then suddenly there came a sense of no longer being alone. I did not hear a voice with my ears, but in my heart I heard clearly, *I have told you to love me with all your strength, and all your heart and all your mind! Trust me. Keep on coming. Ask every question you have, and all will come clear. I love you.* This encounter did not end the questioning. It was not the last time of fear. But it was enough to keep me on the road.

WHAT IS FAITH?

The dilemma was further resolved when I attended an Episcopal conference held at Hood College in Frederick, Maryland, that we called "The Hood Conference." The keynote speaker was a lovely woman, filled with wonderfully irreverent, intellectually-informed and joyous faith. Her name was Marianne Micks. She was the only woman on the faculty at Virginia Theological Seminary. She introduced her talk by saying that she would give us the basis for a liberated theology. The words that came next echoed in my head and heart for the entire week of the conference, and many times since: *Faith is not giving assent to a series of propositions, but saying 'Yes' to the gift and the giver.*

This was a truly liberating message. It freed me from compulsive searches for *the truth* and allowed me simply to encounter God. It helped me to come to the realization that faith is not synonymous with belief—it is rather synonymous, at least in one sense, with commitment and decision, for faith requires an act of the will. In this sense I agree with the evangelical branch of Christianity which pushes for a *decision for Christ*. Where we may differ is that I see this not as a one-time event, but rather as a repeated act in which one engages over and over, if not daily. Done once or daily, a faith commitment would be unnecessary with certainty and proof. But I *choose* to live in a universe populated by the God I am coming to love more and more every day, and *that* demands that I will to have faith.

Jerome Kodell, Abbot of Subiaco Abbey in western Arkansas, uses an image of the spiritual journey as walking forward into the darkness holding a candle. The light on the path ahead is very dim; there is only enough light to walk a step or two. But if one turns around and looks at the path which one has traveled, that is lit by a floodlight! So the faithfulness of God on the journey to the present is a source of deepened faith as we walk into the darkness ahead.

Another meaning of faith is trust. The little child does not have scientific proof of a parent's love, but in their living together day-by-day trust develops. It is not something one *has* as a possession, but something one lives into as a result of experience. Therein lies a paradox. Faith is both a gift and a free choice. You make the choice first, and *then* you are able to experience the gift. (In that sense, it is like any gift—you come to appreciate it fully only after you have received it, have come to use and love it, and have made it truly your own.) The gift is something I can receive gratefully, or which I can refuse. One other way to say this is that faith is not belief *that*, but belief *in*—It is trust.

My prayer for you is that you get past your fears—of loss of control, of conflict between intellect and faith, and of whatever else you fear—and that you come to choose to trust in the God who is calling you and loving you more than you can possibly imagine.

Discoveries About the Spiritual Journey

MAKING THE STORY YOUR OWN

◆ What issues in your background have made faith hard for you? How have you come to understand those issues now?

◆ What definitions have you given to the word *faith* during your lifetime? Write them out and think about the implications of each. Which one(s) work for you now?

◆ When have you felt conflict between faith and belief? Does Marianne Micks' definition of faith provide any solution for you?

◆ St. Paul said, "You are saved by grace through faith" (Eph 2:8). What does this mean to you? How have you experienced it?

◆ If thinking does not solve your dilemmas, try asking God to give you faith. Ask God to show you just one next step.

FOR FURTHER READING

Boulad, Henri. 1991. *All is Grace: God and the Mystery of Time*. New York: Crossroad.

Hurnard, Hannah. 1986. *Hinds Feet on High Places*. Wheaton, IL: Tyndale House.

See also the following scriptural references: Matthew 8: 5-13; Romans 1:16-17; Ephesians 3: 14-21; 1 Thessalonians 1:2-3; Hebrews 11:1-12: 3; James 2: 14-26.

Discoveries About the Spiritual Journey

Revelation Three: Conversion is Putting God in the Center

Original Sin: One's Self Being The Center Of The Universe

My definition of original sin is perceiving myself as the absolute center of the universe with everything and everyone else being an instrument to meet *my* needs. This includes God, to whom I turn to as a last resort fixer when I cannot handle things myself. (An irreverent way to put this is seeing God as "the big Excedrin in the sky.")

The purest example of this kind of self-centeredness that I've seen is found in a scene from the film *The Last Ten Days of Hitler*. In the bunker, just before Hitler and Eva Braun take their cyanide capsules, Hitler is ruminating about the war and says, "I've known for the last two years that we would lose the war."

Eva Braun looks at him in horror, as if she is truly seeing him for the first time and asks, "If you've known that, then *WHY DIDN'T YOU STOP ALL THE KILLING?!!*"

Hitler looks back at her in confusion, at first not understanding the question. Then he responds, "Don't you understand? I had to work out my *destiny!*"

We are all sometimes like that. And each of us sometimes confronts the totally self-centered one inside ourselves that is willing to take out an entire culture to work out our destiny, to save our job, to hold on to our reputation. Sometimes it isn't even such a big price—we'll even do it for a chocolate sundae, or to avoid the bother of recycling, or to have chrome on our cars, or green grass in our yards, or for other such trivia.

My own confrontation with the evil within has happened several times, one of which I will tell you about, because it demolished for me forever the notion that I am at heart a "nice" person. I had worked for a number of years with a colleague with whom I could not get along. It was a very difficult situation for a complex of reasons. First, we shared the same goals and values: we taught together in an undergraduate social work program in a state university, trying to produce graduates who would be competent, caring social workers. We shared commitments to ending racism and gender discrimination in our school, in social agencies, and in society. We had shared commitments to teaching social work as an effective problem-solving profession that looks at issues in a systemic way and comes up with creative responses.

Second, our job descriptions were interconnected in such a way that much of what each of us had to do was dependent on the other's work. Thus it was impossible to be autonomous and just ignore each other.

Discoveries About the Spiritual Journey

Third, the student body was composed of mostly working class White youngsters and inner city Blacks (about in the proportions found in our part of the world at that time—ninety percent Caucasian, ten percent African American). These young adults came with values that made them unlikely to view each other spontaneously as colleagues and friends.

Fourth, there were few women on our school's faculty, and the position of those few was very uncomfortable. My colleague and I both perceived lots of people out there looking for ways to prove that having more women on the faculty would not be productive.

Into that environment, at my behest, our department hired my colleague, who was not only female, but also the only African American faculty member in the school at the time. After just a short time, it became clear that in spite of our common values and aspirations for the program, we pushed each other's worst buttons! I began to feel that no matter what I did, it was wrong. If I was kind, I was perceived as being patronizing. If I was firm, I was perceived as being racist. If I made decisions and presented them, I was excluding her from the process. If I tried to work things out together with her, we ended up at an impasse. If I offered her the decision-making responsibility, I was accused of avoiding it myself. I lost sleep, felt guilty and hypocritical, and was generally miserable. (To give you a sense of how painful this was, part of the reason I went off to do doctoral work was to get away from what felt like an untenable situation, yet one from which, because I loved teaching, I was unwilling to walk away.)

With this background, let me tell you how I learned about the evil inside. My colleague and I had been at loggerheads over the schedule for the following year and ended up bringing this to the department chair. To have to do so went against the grain for both of us: two women arguing and having to take it to a man to settle. It seemed to make us fit into all the stereotypes we hated. And then, in spite of my having presented a "perfect" plan, the department chair decided to accept my *colleague's* proposal!

And I, the professional, adult woman that I was, totally contrary to everything I could will, began to cry! My colleague leaned over, put her

19

hand on my leg, and said in a saccharine voice, "Lynn, dear, is there anything I can do to help?"

I do not remember how I extricated myself from the meeting. I do remember driving home. And I remember experiencing a period of about ten seconds of pure and total hatred. This was followed by the horrifying realization that if no one could ever know the causal connection, and that if I had the power to snap my fingers to make her dead, that I would have done it! At that point I happened to catch a glimpse of my own two eyes in the rear view mirror, and there he was—Adolph Hitler—looking back at me. The only difference between us was that he had sufficient support staff to pull it off with impunity and I didn't. I pulled off the road, breathless. It was the absolute death of my innocence, and a major step on the spiritual journey.

CONVERSION: PUTTING GOD IN THE CENTER

If original sin is putting myself at the absolute center of the universe, with everything and everyone else an instrument to do my will, then conversion is putting God at the center of the universe, and thenceforth viewing everything and everyone, including myself, as an instrument to do God's will.

A friend of mine who was a psychotherapist and writer entered a religious community, one that spends most of its time in silence. I asked him what had drawn him there, and he said, "Each of us is born with a gaping hole inside. It calls out to be filled up. Some of us fill it with alcohol, others with food, others with relationships or work or possessions or experiences or coin collections. We are capable of enormous creativity in finding things with which to fill it. We can even get addicted to lettuce!

"The problem is that whatever we stuff into the hole, doesn't work. It either makes us sick, or does damage to someone or something else, or both. There is only one thing that will fill the hole in a 'whole' way, namely God. The monk is the one who knows this, and who commits to keeping the space empty and available for God, who *will* come from time to time, but will not keep us feeling full all the time."

I quietly replied, "That is true for all of us."

He said, "Yes, but it is a lot easier to consciously keep the space empty when you are in a monastery."

St. Augustine said, "Our hearts are restless until they find their rest in Thee." Getting ourselves out of the center, then getting all the stuff we stuff into it out of the center, and then learning to rest in the emptiness until God fills us, is the task of the journey. Gerald May talks about this at length in his wonderful book *Addiction and Grace*.

There is more to it, however. I believe that conversion has at least two stages. In the first we come to God out of our need, recognizing—however that happens—that we cannot make it without God. But then, gradually, as we live more and more in communion with God, we come to take God's will as our own, and to become truly instruments to do God's will.

I made a retreat many years ago with Fr. John Hugo, a wonderful old Roman Catholic diocesan priest from Pittsburgh. His retreat, called "Encounter with Silence," was also an encounter with the uncompromising need to put God above all things. This is nothing new. We say it blithely in so many ways, and summarize it in both the Hebrew and Christian scriptures in these words: "You shall love the Lord your God with all your heart and with all your soul and with all your mind and with all your strength." But sometimes you need to hear things in a different way to really hear them. Fr. Hugo said it in dozens of new ways, the most powerful of which for me was, "Telling God that you love God more than sin is like telling a beautiful woman that you love her more than toads. God wants you to love God more than anything!"

That is another way to define conversion: to love God more than anything—more than chocolate, more than sex, more than your baseball card collection, more than Hearts on the computer, more than the mountains of Colorado, more than your very own life. And learning to untwine the little tendrils of attachment that hold us to all these things, to free up the interior space for God, is a lifelong task.

John of the Cross talks about "a bird held by a single thread." Even if all other attachments have been sundered, if there is even a little thread still tied around its foot, it cannot fly. I have said that I don't have to worry about a single thread; I have a cable that would hold up the Brooklyn Bridge! But you start where you are—with the loose thread that you can see on the outside of the cable. The others will untwine in their own time. Be gentle with yourself. On the other hand, also be relentless with yourself. Stay on the journey, for you will surely go backward if you do not go forward.

My favorite scriptural statement of the process of conversion is taken from the fifth verse of the twenty-seventh Psalm:

One thing have I asked of You; one thing I seek:
That I might dwell in the House of God for ever.

Living in the House of God means following the customs of the house, which boils down to loving God, self and neighbor. And it means always being "home," it means knowing one is welcome, and that one must welcome all others. It means letting go of the things that are not fitting in the House of God. And it partakes of the flavor of paradox because we are there from the moment of our birth, yet we are also exiles, pilgrims on the journey back.

A friend and co-worker of mine taught me several important lessons in ways that I could hear them. One, perhaps the most important, had to do with being clear about one's goal. John made it a habit before any undertaking, large or small, to stop and remind himself of his goal. Then any activity which took him toward the goal was to be undertaken; any activity, no matter how delightful, which took him away from the goal, was to be abandoned, or at least postponed. This advice is applicable in large and small ways in my life, from the goal of my free afternoon to the goal of eating, the goal of my work (or a particular piece of it), the goal of my marriage, and certainly to the goal of my spiritual pilgrimage and my prayer life.

If I apply this to dwelling in the House of God, many seeming complications of life dissipate. With any activity, I can ask myself: "Is this something that will help me to dwell in the House of God?" If the activity is something that I should do, but don't really want to, I can help by reminding myself that it is not undertaken to punish myself, or for any of a number of other phony reasons, but because I have come to believe it really will take me to (or keep me in) the House of God. Then I can undertake it with a total devotion and a peaceful heart. I have learned that the letting go is not punishment, but gift. I put it thus:

PURIFICATION IS

Letting go
Of burdens
That previously felt
Like a part of the self.

One last thought: sometimes we are not clear on the goal, but have a strong sense that something is right, nonetheless. A way to get at the goal is to fill the in the blanks: I want to do _____ so that _____. If the second blank isn't filled in with what feels like the goal, move it to the first blank and try again. For example:

I want to exercise so that *I look better.*

I want to look better so that *I attract other people.*

Getting this far, I realize the motive for exercise is not taking me to the House of God. But even discounting this motive, exercise feels right, and lots of folks tell me it is important, so I try again.

I want to exercise so that *I am stronger and healthier.*

I want to be strong and healthier so that *I can do the work God has given me to do.*

This is more like it! And I have learned that while my motives are almost always mixed, I can be patient with myself if the intention is to please and serve God. (I believe it was Thomas Merton who once said "Lord, give us the patience to bear with our imperfections until the time is ripe for us to let them go.")

Let me add one more thing about the goal. It is not just an individual thing. All of creation exists for the goal—to glorify God, to please God.

Revelations on the Road

Teillard de Chardin believed that all of creation is engaged in an evolution of consciousness that eventually will lead to a re-union with the source of all consciousness. I do not understand how it might happen, but am coming to believe that he is right, and that my own personal evolution in consciousness both participates in this and contributes to it, whether I know it or not.

An entry from my journal that reflects this says:

I gradually come to see the pattern of life in a much more peaceful way—nature pushing up through the soil of matter with consciousness, then self-consciousness taking over, daring, sloughing off, and (if we are blessed) becoming one with You. Death loses its sting and the down spots are educational experiences. I pray that You be with me, that I know Your Presence now-by-now all my days, that I may walk in keeping with Your will, further the spread of Your kin-dom and witness Your light to those in darkness. I ask in Jesus' name. Amen.

MAKING THE STORY YOUR OWN

◆ Think of a time when you were confronted with something that made you recognize your own self-centeredness. Write about it in your journal. How did you feel? How have you made peace with it? Could you profit from a dialog between the part of yourself that is self-centered and the part that judges her/him?

◆ How would you define conversion for yourself? (Use your own words, those of scripture, or those of a favorite author or speaker that have struck you as worthy.)

◆ Are you aware of addictions that keep you from allowing yourself to be transformed? (One way to define an addiction is "anything you believe you must have in order to allow yourself to be happy" Keyes, 1990.) It could be a person, a possession, a state of being

Discoveries About the Spiritual Journey

(e.g. healthy), or any condition or experience you feel you *must* have. Make a list of such addictions.

◆ Make a list of the ways in which each addiction hinders you from becoming what God calls you to become. Then brainstorm ways you might be freed of each. Pray for God to guide you toward freedom.

FOR FURTHER READING

Bonhoeffer, Dietrich. 1995. *The Cost of Discipleship*. New York: Simon and Schuster.

Evely, Louis. 1963. *That Man is You*. New York: Paulist Press.

Finley, James. 1980. *Merton's Palace of Nowhere*. Notre Dame, IN: Ave Maria Press.

Hillesum, Etty. 1996. *Etty Hillesum : An Interrupted Life the Diaries, 1941-1943 and Letters from Westerbork*. New York: Henry Holt.

May, Gerald. 1991. *Addiction and Grace*. San Francisco: HarperSanFrancisco.

Yungblut, John. 1994. *The Gentle Art of Spiritual Guidance*. Rockport, MA: Element.

PART 2:
Struggles and Signposts From My Life on the Road

Struggles and Signposts From My Life on the Road

Revelation Four: Being A Woman Matters

Learning And Unlearning How To Be A Woman

Every woman has a story about learning what it means to be a woman. The story includes funny things, joyful things, and painful things, in varying proportions for each of us. Compared to many others, my woman story is pale. I have not been raped; I have not been sexually abused; I have been sexually harassed, but not to a degree or at a time in my life when it could seriously damage me. Furthermore, I have not experienced some things that for many women are the core experiences of womanhood: pregnancy, childbirth, nursing and raising children. Yet I too have a woman story.

Revelations on the Road

Born in 1942, I am in the generation of women raised before the later 20th Century women's movement, but irrevocably changed by it in young adulthood. I can trace the change simply by looking at my own writing. In college I used the generic "man" not only without shame or discomfort, but even without awareness that there was another option. It astonishes me when I read it now. I am also stung by the retrospective awareness I now have of the unconscious yet all-pervasive sexism in almost all the songs of my teenage years that I thought were so wonderful at the time. There were no women there: only *baby dolls* and *girls*.

I was raised by a competent, self-confident, educated woman who did not work for pay outside the home while I was growing up, but who was fully engaged in highly professional volunteer work. She went off for graduate education while I was getting my own and worked for pay for a number of years thereafter. She was outraged by the principal of my high school telling her that I didn't need a third year of a foreign language (a strongly suggested prerequisite for admission to my college of choice at the time), because I was a girl and didn't need formal education. She gave me a model for being a woman that I could, and still can, embrace without ambivalence.

Another gift that came as I was trembling on the threshold between girlhood and womanhood happened in a flash during my sixth grade year. I didn't fully appreciate its meaning or power at the time, but have revisited it over and over, and believe now that I was saved from a long detour that most girls of my age and social class were forced to take. Carol Gilligan, in her landmark book on women's development entitled *In A Different Voice*, has reported that little girls at the time of puberty desert their own inner wisdom in droves, being taught by society to trust others, especially male others, more than themselves. One man choose to teach the opposite.

Mr. Pompiani was my first male teacher. He came along in sixth grade, just when I needed him. He was handsome and smart. I had just reached the age where crushes were possible, and I developed a big one on Mr. Pompiani, though I doubt that he was aware of it. I wanted him to think I was smart, and I wanted him to approve of me. I wanted that a lot.

30

One day in our arithmetic class Mr. Pompiani told us that zero divided by one was zero. In fact zero divided by anything was zero. The next day he asked us to speculate on what one divided by zero might be. Without much hesitation, twenty-nine of thirty little sixth grade voices chanted "zee-row"! Mr. Pompiani looked around and asked, "Does everyone agree with this?"

I was sitting in my first row seat feeling uneasy. I understood what division was-seeing how many times one number could "fit" into another. I tried to imagine slipping zero into one, and it was so tiny it kept disappearing. I felt a little strange, almost dizzy, as it slipped in without making any difference, over and over again. Finally in a *very* little voice I said, "I don't know, but I think it's big."

Mr. Pompiani looked at me in surprise and asked, "Does anyone agree with Lynn?" I looked around the rest of the room, and all I saw were twenty-nine sixth grade heads shaking "No." Then Mr. Pompiani turned to me and asked me what may be the most important question anyone has ever asked of me (with the possible exception of the ones I have answered at Baptism and Marriage with the words, "I do"). His question was "Do you want to change your answer?"

I did want to change my answer. It felt pretty cold and lonely out there on the tree branch. But something inside me could not deny my vision of that zero slipping over and over into the one. So I shook my head and, in a very, very, *very* small voice said, "No."

Mr. Pompiani then did something amazing. He took about a minute and a half to explain infinity, and the rest of the class hour to state and elaborate on the fact that one person could be right and everybody else wrong. I have never forgotten it. I learned that this funny sensation of seeing something strange and new could be trusted. My mind could be trusted. My heart could be trusted. I could trust myself and my own inner wisdom.

Years later I went to an all-women's college (Barnard) where the model of superwoman was presented as the norm. (The president of the school had married at 39, had had five children, and had become president of the school, in addition to many other achievements.) I took her as a model for myself.

Whatever oppression I had experienced had been largely unconscious. The consciousness-raising did not come all at once.

Here are some of the events that, as I look back on them, mark my reaching new levels of understanding.

◆ I graduated from Barnard College with a degree in Sociology and a respectable quality point average. Then I was asked in my first job interview at an advertising agency (where I aspired to become a market analyst) if I could type and take shorthand. I walked out and didn't try that career line again.

◆ I came to realize that the motivation for all my romances was not what it seemed, but that as a woman, therefore as one often dis-counted by men, I could at least get their attention by being the object of their romantic interest. This allowed at least the illusion of reciprocal intimacy.

The realization, when it came, was a loss as well as a gain. I could never again surrender innocently to the urge to sexualize a rela-tionship for that goal. Here is how it came out in poem-form:

FROM FISHER TO FRUIT TREE

As a child I learned
From my love-hunger
How to get love
By being lovable, but I forgot it.

As a teenager I learned
From my love-hunger
How to get love
By being sexy.
I never forgot it.

As a young woman I learned
Sex wasn't love.

But not knowing otherway to get love
I got very sexy.

As a mature woman I learned
I could use sexy as an introduction for loving.
It wasn't perfect
But it was better than before.

I am just starting to learn
I don't need to be loved by everyone
Because I am loved by God and by my self,
And am abundantly blessed with love from others.

I am also learning
To see love not as the fisher's bait
Thrown forth in exaltation
And reeled back in to feed my needs;
Rather to give as the apple tree gives apples,
With no strings attached
Seeking nothing
Because it knows its fulfillment is to give.

And the scattered seeds bring forth more loving trees.
Amen.

◆ When I started teaching, I was confronted at the first faculty event—an event to which faculty spouses were not invited—by a man who remarked, "Oh, you must be the new token woman!" I do not remember what I answered. It was something like "I'm not a token anything; I'm the very best there is." But I have wished ever since for a response that would have merited inclusion in *The Saturday Evening Post* as "the perfect squelch."

I spent over a year trying to convince the dean of our school at the university that it was not "cute" to remark on the quality of my figure or legs. It ended when, after a period of "remission" that had lulled me into the comfortable illusion that he was cured, he came into my office one day where I was sitting in a skirt with my legs crossed, and said, "Isn't that a pretty picture."

I exploded from the chair and walked quickly toward him. With high heels on, I was slightly taller than he, and I backed him across the hall and up against the wall. From less than a foot away, with students in the hall during change of class, in my deepest and loudest voice I bellowed, "When are you going to get it through your f-ing head that I find that f- ing offensive?!!!" The color drained from his face and he stammered "I . . . I . . . I think I just did!" He slithered along against the wall to the door of his office and never bothered me again. Furthermore, he never in any way of which I was aware, did anything in retaliation. This makes me think he really had been oblivious to the effect of his behavior on me. But what a lot of energy for both of us to have had to expend on something that should have been obvious! (This was the first and last time I ever used the "f-word" in a professional setting.)

◆ On a retreat I was led in a guided meditation in which God was a large-breasted woman who nursed me.

At first I was shocked, then overwhelmed with the wonder and giftedness of my position.

◆ I experienced a woman priest celebrating Holy Communion for the first time.

I was in a diocese that did not ordain women. In fact the Standing Committee (an elected group of clergy and laity with the power to deny ordination) had developed a written and public statement to the effect that they did not believe women to be fit candidates for ordination to the priesthood. They said that this statement was being offered for pastoral reasons to prevent women from applying and being disappointed.

So I was not expecting to find a woman celebrant at a Eucharist in our diocese. Furthermore I had known in advance that her name was Beryl Choi, and I had expected her to be male, and Asian to boot. She was instead a Caucasian woman.

When I saw her, vested, standing behind the altar, I felt surprise. In fact, something in my body made a profound shift. When she began the prayer of consecration, I heard what sounded like the wail of a wounded moose. It was me, sobbing, from some place deep within. It continued (though with a much lower decibel level) throughout the rest of the service. It did not make rational sense; no person is Christ. But I felt represented before God and community in a way I never had before—had not even known I was missing. I have never forgotten it.

Given what I have been privy to of women's struggles in the process toward ordination, I am grateful that I have not been called to that form of ministry. But I am indescribably grateful that some women have been called, and have had the courage to say their "yes."

◆ God's feminine aspects were brought powerfully home to me in a lecture by Phyllis Trible (a feminist theologian and scripture scholar). Among other things, she told us that the word "created" as in "God created the heavens and the earth" (Gn 1:1) can only be literally translated from the Hebrew as the physical act of giving birth, certainly a feminine thing to do.

Trible called this, and other sections of scripture, *subversive texts*— texts that, in spite of the all-powerful and all-pervasive patriarchy of the time in which they were written, clearly conveyed the truth of God's love for the feminine as well as the masculine, for God's partaking of the nature of feminine as well as masculine, and for God's love of particular women as well as men.

◆ I noticed myself becoming not angry, but saddened, by women who prefer to be called "chairmen" of committees, even in the years after most other women's consciousness had been irrevocably raised.

Revelations on the Road

◆ I was stunned by a film from the Canadian film board entitled *The Burning Times* which recorded in a powerful documentary format the destruction in Europe, between the years of 1100 and 1900, of as many as 9 million persons, most of whom were women, who had been identified by the inquisition as witches or heretics.

Whole villages were destroyed. After a person was subjected to the first, second, and, if necessary "third degree" of torture; she was required, in proving the sincerity of her confession, to name names. Many of these women had been healers: midwives and herbalists. They were now a threat to the newly university-educated, male doctors. Healing by non-university-trained persons (i.e. women) was thenceforth defined as witchcraft.

I saw this film at a retreat for women "dancing on the edge," where forty two women grieved together over their collective experience of injustice in the Church and society, and rejoiced together in signs of hope we see for the future.[1]

◆ The last factor I'll tell you about in my consciousness-raising is the reading of lots and lots of books.

I shall mention only two. First is *Against Our Will* by Susan Brownmiller. It is a study of the systematic use of rape throughout human history to control women and humiliate their men. (I have also read and heard parallel stories of foot-binding in China, of genital mutilation in Africa, of widow-burning in India, and of more, which, while not about rape, reinforce the notion that women have been used throughout history by men simply as objects to fulfill men's objectives.)

The second book is *The Sacred Dimensions of Women's Experience*, edited by Elizabeth Dodson Gray. This anthology of stories of women who participated in a Harvard seminar is presented in sections on such topics as childbirth, the art of cooking, the art of creating order and beauty in a home, creativity, and friendship. It is a gentle, powerful, feminist presentation of the gifting God gives particularly to women. It deeply affirmed me, called me to new insights, and offered me some models for wholeness.

One day at a conference in a large hotel I was gifted with a sudden and intense awareness of how much I valued my sisters. It emerged as this poem:

My Sisterhood

I celebrate the women
With their ripe, outrageous, proud voluptuousness
Striding through the hallways of my hotel.
Black wearing purple, green and red;
Blonde wearing pink and mauve;
Scarves fluttering, silent rhythms swirling;
Energy and power discovered and claimed.

They call to me
(Without words or glances)
"Isn't it wonderful
Just
Being
Us?"

I discovered in the process of writing this chapter that we had not made as much progress as I thought, when listening one day to the radio I heard a comedienne talk about other women:

"All my friends are men. Women are always competing with you, and offering you advice on how to look better: 'Wear clogs and black socks with your evening gown; looks great!'"

I didn't know whether to be shocked, saddened, angry or all three.

I didn't know which was worse: that she had said it, or that a male disc jockey had found it funny enough to use for his "One minute humor break." I recognized in me the self that had been nourished and affirmed, over and over again, by the tender love of women, and yearned for the day when that would be the primary experience all of us have of one another.

This is not an impossible dream. I have had it upon many occasions. One of the gifts of middle age in this time and place is that women, at least the women I have been blessed to meet, are more and more capable of setting aside the competitive conditioning they experienced in childhood and of finding ways to nurture and support each other on their spiritual journeys. (Some men are also finding gifts in learning about and from this process.)

It was perhaps most wonderfully true for me at a women's retreat in Tennessee several years ago, and resulted in the following poem which I wrote and shared with the other participants:

You

You are Palpable.

I move through You
With every step.

You move through me
With every breath.

You shine behind my eyes
And in hers
(All the here-hers)
Who Grace me with their Presence
Who show You forth in some
Of Your infinite Variety.

And yet You are Beyond—so far Beyond . . .
Yonder.

From within and from without
You feed me

With hunger
For You
Mother-Mine.
And I am . . .how to say it . . .
I Am in
Intense
Peace.

Amen

MAKING THE STORY YOUR OWN

◆ Where are the benchmarks on your path of raising consciousness about "the woman thing"? (Men are allowed to answer this, and the following questions, as well. It might be intriguing to try to answer them with the "feminine voice within.")

◆ How have you come to experience the feminine face of God? Is it as nursing mother (see Ps 131); as a mother hen (Mt 23:37)? Or is there another image that speaks powerfully to your experience?

◆ Take the image you discovered in the last exercise and sit with it in prayer. Let Her speak to you the word you most need to hear. Then be still. Give thanks before you leave the holy place where you encountered Her.

◆ I recently got a book entitled *Women Make the Best Friends*. Is this true in your experience? What particular qualities of character do you find in women friends that makes you value them? Can you find these qualities also in yourself?

◆ For men only: Give a name to "the woman within" and write a dialogue with her. Begin by asking her "Who are you, and what do you have to say to me?" Let the dialogue unfold. When it feels finished,

Revelations on the Road

ask one more question: "What gift do you have for me?" Close
with a prayer of thanksgiving.

◆ For women only: Give a name to "the man within" and write a
dialogue with him. Begin by asking him "Who are you, and what
do you have to say to me?" Let the dialogue unfold. When it feels
finished, ask one more question: "What gift do you have for me?"
Close with a prayer of thanksgiving.

FOR FURTHER READING

Anderson, Sherry R. and Patricia Hopkins. 1991. *The Feminine Face of
God: The Unfolding of the Sacred in Women.* New York: Bantam.

Bohlen, Jean Shinolda. 1994. *Crossing to Avalon: A Woman's Midlife
Pilgrimage.* San Francisco: HarperSanFrancisco.

Brownmiller, Susan. 1993. *Against Our Will: Men, Women and Rape.*
Greenwich, CT: Fawcett.

Gilligan, Carol. 1993. *In A Different Voice: Psychological Theory and
Women's Development.* Cambridge: Harvard University Press.

Gray, Elizabeth Dodson.Ed. 1988. *Sacred Dimensions of Women's
Experience.* Wellesley, MA: Roundtable Press.

Wise, Lois. 1994. *Women Make the Best Friends.* New York: Simon and
Schuster.

Revelation Five: Dealing with The *Why* Question

I have received many gifts from my Jewish heritage. One of those is an intimate acquaintance with what I have come to call the *Why* question. For several years prior to my birth in 1942, my mother had worked as a social worker assisting Jewish refugees to resettle in our town. I do not remember overhearing any discussions about World War II or about Hitler, but they must have taken place, as I do remember a repetitive nightmare I had at about the age of three. Night after night, a man I identified by the name of Hitler was driving a bulldozer, pushing up a huge pile of dirt and trying to bury me

Revelations on the Road

alive. There was a relentless, implacability about this—I was going to die! While there may be other implications of this dream, I am most struck by the fact that the horror of the Holocaust emerged in the dream of a three-year-old who was almost totally insulated in her day-to-day life from its direct consequences.

I have been fascinated with the Holocaust ever since. I remember being in awe of Mr. Silberman, a German-Jewish refugee who had owned a number of shoe factories in pre-war Germany, and who had come here without English, after having spent time first in a forced labor camp and later in a concentration camp. Having no English, he accepted a position as janitor at our temple, and turned the job into one of great dignity, influence and respect. He had a deep, centered spirituality; simply being in his presence made me feel very safe. I trusted Mr. Silberman and intuitively knew I could learn a lot from him.

When I was a teenager, the Israelis arrested and tried Adolf Eichmann. I was filled with righteous indignation at Eichmann's crimes against humanity, and couldn't wait to get to temple to ask Mr. Silberman what he thought should be done to Eichmann. I had been thinking up my own most imaginative varieties of torture as possible punishments. Mr. Silberman looked at me with big, sad brown eyes and in his accented English softly said, "I think it is time that someone has the courage and wisdom to say that there has been enough killing." I was humbled. I sat there for a little while, then got up and silently walked away.

I have read a lot about the Holocaust, trying somehow to come to an understanding of what could make people treat each other like that. And I have found myself facing the same evil, in other guises, in direct or indirect confrontations with such phenomena as the Civil Rights struggle, the holocausts perpetrated by "Americans" against Native Americans, the Pol Pot regime against the Cambodian people, and ethnic groups against each other in such diverse locations as Bosnia, Ireland, the Middle East, Rwanda and Sierra Leone, El Salvador, and the Philippines.

One can look at this from a number of perspectives. Some things do "make sense" in a bizarre sort of way. The evil I deny within myself gets projected onto others, both individually and corporately. The effort to expunge it from my own unconscious results in my killing the one upon whom I have projected it and who now represents it for me. One can see the holocausts as the fulfillment of absolute self-centeredness, seen most starkly in the movie *The Last Ten Days of Hitler* (see the story on page 18), and in less dramatic ways when we are willing to buy products we know are manufactured under conditions harmful to other people or to our environment.

This view of the problem of evil, where we examine the behavior of the perpetrator (ourselves or others), remains somehow more in our head than in our heart and gut. But when we are the victim, or where we identify primarily with the victim, it moves rapidly into the place where we live emotionally. Then we turn to God and scream, "Why?"; "Why me?"; "Why do you allow this?"; "What did I do to make it happen?"; "When will it end?"; "What is its meaning?"; or simply, "Oh, God, *why?*"

THERE IS NO ANSWER TO THE *WHY* QUESTION

I have come to the conclusion that, on the face of the earth, there is no satisfactory answer to the *Why* question. It is not found in any philosophy, in any of the world's religions, or in any other source I have examined. There are those who think they have the answer. If you examine the story of Job, you will find that Job's so-called friends were sure of the answer. Whether or not he was aware of it, they knew he had sinned and was being punished by a just, if not merciful, God. But those of us privy to "the rest of the story" know that that was not the case. And the Job story has never satisfied me. My summary of the plot line is:

Job: Oh, God, why?
God: It's none of your business; I'm God and you're not.
Job: You're right, I'm sorry.
God: That's all right.
     The end.

Revelations on the Road

Perhaps others are satisfied by this. I am not.

I have a friend who believes in reincarnation who told me that the answer to the *Why* question is found in the concept of karma. Bad things happen here because of negative energy carried over from bad things in a previous life that need to be worked out here. I asked, "Well then, why did the bad things happen in the previous life?" He looked at me in surprise and said, "I don't know." It seems to me that several lifetimes of "bad things" are even worse than one! In any case the problem is not solved by the concept of Karma.

I see the resolution in two ways, both admittedly open to modification. First, if I am faced with a choice between living in a world in which lots of bad things happen, and where there is no God, and living in a world in which lots of bad things happen, and where there is a God, I choose the latter. I believe that faith is an ongoing choice, as well as a gift. It does not solve the problem of the *Why* question, but it does help me survive in the midst of the dilemma.

While the story of Job does not give me much help in answering the *Why* question another story in the Bible points in a helpful direction. (Note that the disciples in this story lived with the same assumptions as did Job's friends.)

> *As (Jesus) walked along, he saw a man blind from birth. His disciples asked him, "Rabbi, who sinned, this man or his parents, that he was born blind?" Jesus answered, "Neither this man nor his parents sinned' he was born blind so that God's works might be revealed in him"* (Jn 9:2-3).

Jesus goes on to heal the man. This incident leads us to a second question.

THE SECOND QUESTION: WHAT CAN I DO WITH IT, NOW THAT I'VE GOT IT?

It seems to me that we, as human beings, are built with a need to ask the *Why* question. We ask it whenever something bad happens which does not make sense to us. But after a certain amount of time, if we are wise, we come to the conclusion that there is no answer, and we let go of the question. Sometimes we let go because we are too bloodied to ask it any more, sometimes just because we are too tired, and sometimes because the pain has made us wise.

Whatever leads us there, at that letting-go point, there is another question to which I believe there is always an answer, if we ask it willing to hear it. The second question is: "What can I do with it, now that I've got it?" In fact the worse the situation provoking the *Why* question, the more powerfully redemptive is the potential answer to this second question. Those I have known who have had terrible "its" (as in "why did it happen to me"), and who have asked the second question, have had opportunities to witness faith, hope and courage that are often life-changing for others.

Let me share one such witness. One of my closest friends, Clair, died of metastatic breast cancer in 1994. Prior to her illness, she and I had talked about what would happen if our husbands both predeceased us. We thought this was possible because first, women live longer than men, and second, we took better care of ourselves than did our husbands. We made a tentative commitment to living together in late life, and to starting a small, non-traditional religious community. In our home there would be private spaces for each member, and shared public spaces. Members would have some shared ministry, prayer and communal life, and some time that could be spent in solitude.

Clair had a mastectomy in 1992, followed by what we both thought was successful chemotherapy. When she learned in 1993 that her cancer had not only returned but had spread widely in her body, she called me to say that she had "good news and bad news." I asked for the bad news first, and she replied, "I will have to back out of our commitment to live together in late life." As I realized the import of what she had said, I asked, "And the *good* news?" "I'll be there to welcome you when you come over," she replied.

45

As the time for her death approached, Clair told me that her last ministry was to teach those who were providing care for her how to die with grace and faith. That is an answer to what I now call "the second question" —what can I do with it now that I've got it? Her willingness and graced ability to ask this question allowed even her death to be used for good.

If we are honest with ourselves, the *Why* question simply amounts to "Why can't things be the way I/we want them?" When we read the stories of others who go through bad things and have the courage to ask the second question, we can wisely nod that we now understand why. But the why was not a given. It was wrestled out of the darkness by the willingness of the sufferer to ask the second question in literally blind faith.

Viktor Frankl was a Jewish psychiatrist interned in a concentration camp during World War II. He lost virtually every living soul he knew. He saw every degradation to which human beings have subjected one another. In the midst of unspeakable horror, Frankl managed not only to survive, but to develop a form of psychotherapy, Logotherapy, which is based on the notion that if we can find sense, or *make* sense out of suffering, then it can be redeemed. Frankl did not believe in bearing suffering unnecessarily. He teaches that the first obligation we have in the face of suffering, our own or that of others, is to end it. But when all our efforts are in vain, there is but one thing left to our freedom. Frankl said it thus: "The final freedom is the freedom to choose one's attitude." [1]

To take a much milder example from everyday life, imagine having a flat tire on your car. You have two choices: you either have a flat tire and have a miserable day because of it, or you have a flat tire and have a nice day anyway. You do not have the choice not to have a flat tire, but you do have a choice about your attitude. I do not believe that I have enough life experience to be able to exhort you to choose your attitude as Frankl did, but he is certainly a trustworthy teacher. So are Clair, and the many models of heroism in your own life.

One of my favorite models is a former client, a twenty-two-year-old woman who in 1969 walked into Family and Child Service where I was a family social worker, and whom I shall call Pat. Pat came without an appointment, sat down, and fixed me with a determined look, saying, "I woke up this morning and decided I'm not going to live this way the rest of my life." I asked what "this way" was, and she shared her agonizing life story with me. Pat was, it appeared, the only non-drinking adult in her everyday world. All the adults with whom she had grown up were active alcoholics. Pat had hoped to escape from that life and had been offered a scholarship to art school, but had gotten pregnant in her junior year of high school and had married the baby's father. In his family, too, every adult was an active alcoholic.

As Pat's story emerged, two conflicting reactions were going on in my heart and mind. Her history would auger poorly for a happy or productive life: there had been too little nurture, a life totally empty of good role models, no support. On the other hand my intuition was saying, "This lady is going to make it!" I agreed to work with her, and we did so for about four months. By the end of that time Pat had a job, was in her own apartment, looked and felt better than she had since her junior year in high school, had hope of some commercial art training to be paid for by her employer, hope of promotion, and some friends who were a lot healthier than either her family or her soon-to-be-former husband.

We terminated work together because we both felt that, at least for the time being, she was ready to go it on her own. Near the end of our last session, I asked her a question I'd had for months: "I knew in my gut when I met you that you were going to be okay. But I honestly don't know how. From everything I know of human behavior, your health and wisdom and strength seem to have developed in a totally hostile desert. Do you have any sense of how this happened, and how I might be able to encourage others based on your story?" She looked all of fifteen years old with her very trim body, and long straight, blond hair hanging to her waist. But her voice was the voice of wisdom, hard-earned but well-learned, as she replied with a slight smile, "Lynn, all I can tell you is that sometimes shit

Revelations on the Road

makes good fertilizer." *That* is what we are called to: to use whatever bad things happen to us as fertilizer, for they are no use for anything else.

This all takes us back to the question we dealt with earlier, the goal of our spiritual journey. If we make our own happiness and satisfaction the goal of our life, if we suffer under the illusion that God is really there primarily to solve our problems as we dictate, then we are going to be terribly disappointed when things go against the direction we most deeply choose. But if we are able to put God in the center of our lives, then we are able to ask the second question. What we are saying really is, "Okay. It isn't what I would have chosen. So how can I take this and use it for God's purposes?" The parent who, out of the ashes of her own child's funeral pyre, starts a program for other parents in grief has asked this question. Clair asked this question. Pat asked this question. And if we would have our griefs redeemed, we must pray that after we have grieved, after we have asked the *Why* question, we have the courage to ask the second question and to be open to the answer.

MAKING THE STORY YOUR OWN

◆ When in your life have you found yourself asking the *Why* question ? What answers have you been able to find that work for you?

◆ Read the story of the man who spent 38 years by a pool waiting to be healed (Jn. 5:1-11). Note that he did not answer Jesus' question, "Do you want to be healed?" Was he perhaps way too committed to his world view? There was no way he could have gotten into the water in time, no matter how long he waited. What must he have been saying to himself? When have you been trapped in a similar pattern? He must say, "I am helpless, Lord. Help me!" We are often like that. (Save us, God, from presumptuous sins!)

◆ In Romans 8:28 Paul says, "We know that in all things God works for good for those who love the Lord." When and how have you found this true in your own experience?

48

Struggles and Signposts From My Life on the Road

FOR FURTHER READING

Bonhoeffer, Dietrich. 1972. *Letters and Papers from Prison.* New York: Macmillan.

Capon, Farrar Robert. 1995. *The Third Peacock.* Published in *The Romance of the Word : One Man's Love Affair With Theology: Three Books.* San Diego, CA: Wm. B. Eerdmans Publishing Co.

De Caussade, Jean-Pierre. 1995. *The Fire of Divine Love: Readings from Jean-Pierre De Caussade.* Translated by Robert Llewelyn. Chicago: Triumph.

Frankl. Viktor. 1997. *Man's Search for Meaning,* Revised and Updated Edition. New York: Washington Square Press.

Green, Thomas, SJ. 1995. *When the Well Runs Dry.* Notre Dame, IN: Ave Maria Press.

Revelation Six: It's All of Us or None

    A few years ago on a visit to New York City I made friends with an old woman on a bus. I noticed she had a brown paper grocery bag on her lap. Noticing my glance, she asked conspiratorially, "Guess what I've got in the bag?" I replied, "I'm afraid you'll have to tell me." She then proudly informed me that she was seventy-eight years old and that in the bag was her recently completed autobiography. She was on her way to Holt, Rinehart and Winston with it, sure that they would be eager to publish it. It

Revelations on the Road

had really written itself, she confessed, and "the only hard part was coming up with a title. For you see I wanted the title to sum up all the wisdom I have gained in my 78 years."

I stopped a moment to think, wondering how I would ever tackle such a chore. Finally I asked, "What ever did you call it?"

With a triumphant smile she exploded, *"It's all of us or none!"*

So You Think You Accept Others, Do You?

One of the most powerful learning experiences I ever had took place in 1957 at a regional youth conference for Jewish teens from the Great Lakes area. The conference was held that year in a small town north of Pittsburgh. Rabbi Falk, the rabbi from my own home congregation, was in charge. We spent Saturday morning talking about what was then called "Brotherhood." We examined racial prejudice and discrimination as it was being modeled in such places as Little Rock, Arkansas and Birmingham, Alabama, and were busy playing "ain't it awful" all morning. Not much different from the little sixth graders in Mr. Pompiani's class, we all made the same noises and shook our heads, full of the security of knowing The Truth. We had the added advantage of feeling morally superior to others, who clearly didn't measure up to our high standards of ethical sensitivity.

At lunch Rabbi Falk announced that he had just looked at the conference registration list and had discovered that we did not have enough boys to make the Saturday night dance a success. He wondered if we would like him to invite Christian boys from one of the local churches to round out our complement of males. We debated it, and did some real soul-searching, for we had come to this conference in part because it was one of the few places in our world where we could immerse ourselves fully in an all—Jewish environment. This was especially true for those of us from towns in which we were very much the minority. But practicality won out, and we finally decided that it would be all right.

Then Rabbi Falk informed us that since this was not his town, he had no way of knowing which of the churches had Negro children and which

52

White. He wondered if that would matter to us. Chaos emerged! Some kids threatened to go home. Others said they would stay, but would boycott the dance. Others would come, but wouldn't have anything to do with "them." Others would talk, but not dance. Everyone drew their own lines. After about half an hour of pandemonium, Rabbi Falk interrupted us with another announcement: he had rechecked, and we *did* have enough boys after all!

We spent the afternoon processing what had just taken place. We went home wiser and sadder and very much humbled. And I learned that while my words and behavior measured up to my own high standards, my feelings assuredly did not!

LOVING REQUIRES KNOWING

It is easy to classify those who are different as "other." It is hard to see them as part of "us" rather than "them" unless we take the time to get to know them. If we do, we discover, sometimes with a shock of surprise, our common humanity. I have been blessed to do this with a number of folks, each of whom has confronted me with another of my previously unrecognized prejudices.

One of my classmates in high school, whom I shall call Janie Smythe, had what we used to call in the 1950's a reputation. I hadn't met her, but I had heard about her! And I had listened to the stories and been amazed at Janie's outrageous behaviors. One day my study hall was overcrowded, so the teacher asked some of us to double up at our desks, which were really big enough to seat two. I sat with a cute, petite, pixie-like girl I had not met before, and somehow we got to talking about reputations. I told her the most outrageous reputation in school belonged to someone I had never met, named Janie Smythe. I proceeded to repeat what I had heard about Janie, even elaborating on it a bit.

You guessed it! As I turned to her in mock outrage and asked, "What do you think of *that?!*", she replied quietly, "Not much. None of it is true. I know

Revelations on the Road

because *I* am Janie Smythe!" I do not remember what I said. I *do* remember the hot shame I felt. I was humbly grateful when she accepted my apology and granted my plea for forgiveness. And I proceeded to learn as much as she could teach me about the horrible power of gossip to destroy.

Galen Buckwalter was a student in the social work program in which I taught. He was a tall, handsome, self-possessed young man with more brains and character than any three people could ever use. He was also a quadriplegic, having broken his spine at the age of seventeen while diving into the Susquehanna River. Galen was fairly self-contained, and I probably would not have gotten to know him if we had not participated together in a workshop designed to break down barriers of all kinds within the university. We were paired together in an exercise to talk about gender and sexuality, and ended up becoming fast friends.

Galen told me his story—took me through the entire experience of diving into the river, being terrified by seeing his own legs on a gurney (legs which, initially he did not even recognize as his own), and spending eight months with a brace attached to his skull, unable to move except as moved by the staff of the hospital. He spoke of the evolution in his attitude toward his body, from initial abhorrence through tolerance to a return to loving the "house" in which he lived. He showed the same determination to care for his body, and to use it maximally, as I had for my own body. He taught me that "no body's perfect", that I am not my body, and perhaps even more important, that it is possible to have peace and true wisdom emerge from the kind of trauma he had experienced.

Prior to getting to know Galen, I had consistently experienced some discomfort when meeting people with obvious physical disabilities. After that experience, the discomfort vanished. I had learned that he (and, by extension, all others with physical challenges) were truly human too. Perhaps I also learned that I, too, am disabled in some ways, less obvious but no less real, and that accepting myself demands acceptance of the learning from my friend on the New York City bus: it's all of us or none.

This same learning happened with a Black woman who graciously shared her story and helped me to understand her experience of discrimination from the inside. It happened again with a gay man. Ron's poetry and patience helped me understand what it is like to grow up in a society where what you experience is viewed with, at best, a lack of understanding, and at worst, genuine abhorrence. And it continues to happen in ways that still take me by surprise. Let me tell you about one of those.

When my husband and I moved to Tennessee, I carried a lot of stereotypes about the South, many of them shaped by my "media-ted" experiences of it during the height of the civil rights struggle. I had no sense of what would prove to be accurate and what was simply my own fantasy. We first lived in Sewanee, Tennessee, a small unincorporated town owned entirely by the University of the South. The town police were the University police.

During our first week there I was stopped for driving at forty miles-per-hour in a twenty mile-per-hour zone near the hospital. My heart rate doubled and my palms began to sweat as I rapidly fantasized my car, with Pennsylvania plates, being found somewhere near my body in a swamp. As the scene flashed through my mind, along with another, of my husband calling the Sewanee police and being told that no one had reported an accident, and that no one had seen my car, the seemingly eight-foot tall policeman approached my car.

He leaned down and said in a very soft, gentle voice, "Ma'am, we are tryin' very hard to get traffic to slow down on Universitah Avenue, and Ah'm wuhndrin' if you could hold it down to, say, thirty." I gulped, replied quickly, "I think I can do that," and gulped again as he turned and walked away. I sat there, stunned at my own prejudice, and then called out after him, "If you ever want anyone to nominate you for the 'Nicest Policeman of the Year Award', call on me."

In addition to making it difficult to love others when we stereotype them, we do damage to ourselves as well. On some very deep level, we

Revelations on the Road

know that we and they are somehow one, and that what we do to them, we do ultimately to ourselves as well. Jesus pointed this out in his inimitable style when he said about the poor, the hungry, the ill, and those in prison, "just as you did it to one of the least of these who are members of my family, you did it to me" (Mt 25:40).

This idea is captured in the prayer used most often by Christians of all varieties all around the world—the Lord's prayer—in the words, "forgive us our trespasses as we forgive those who trespass against us." This does not mean that we are paid back in kind, although many people might interpret it that way. Rather it means that we either believe in the possibility of unearnable forgiveness, available to all persons, including ourselves—or we do not—in which case it applies to no one, not even ourselves. Jesus says, "You have heard that it was said, 'You shall love your neighbor and hate your enemy.' But I say to you, love your enemies and pray for those who persecute you, so that you may be children of your Father in heaven; for he makes his sun rise on the evil and on the good, and sends rain on the righteous and on the unrighteous" (Mt 5:43-44).

My husband illustrates this in a way that delights my heart, in what he calls a true test of "Christianity." Start by assuming that you were a "good Christian"—and you can define that any way you want. For our purposes imagine that you went to church every Sunday. You fasted and prayed; you gave alms; you were kind and loving and honest to everyone. You died and, as expected, went to heaven. The test is, how would you feel if you got there and found *everyone else* there too? I mean *everyone!* I mean Mata Hari and Attila the Hun and anyone in your own life experience whom you were able to tolerate only because you knew it would get you to heaven. If you smiled and reached out to that person and said, "Wow! I didn't expect to find you here. But this is wonderful. We have had our differences, but now we have all eternity to work them out," then you would have passed the test. But if you found your heart shriveled up, unwilling to accept their presence, then *it would be hell!*

Will Campbell, a Southern Baptist preacher from a small town in rural Mississippi, wrote a semi-autobiographical novel entitled *Brother to a Dragonfly,* in which he recounts a story about his coming to this awareness. Campbell went to Yale (or perhaps Harvard), but was never "citified." He worked for decades in the civil rights movement in the South, and also was a personal chaplain to members of the Ku Klux Klan. It is a measure of his ability to accept others where they are that both Blacks and Whites accepted his ministry. I once heard him address a clergy group in Tennessee where he defended this strange ministry by saying, "God didn't say 'Love everybody, 'ceptin' if they're Black.' And God didn't say, 'Love everybody, 'ceptin' if they're Klan.' God just said 'Love everybody.' And after all, who needs to hear what I have to say, *White liberals?!*"

The story he told in his book takes place in Georgia during the height of the civil rights struggle. Campbell had a friend, P.D., an atheist, who often questioned Campbell about being a person of faith. Once he asked for a definition of Christianity in ten words or less. Campbell replied, "I can do it in eight! We're all bastards, but God loves us anyway." He went on to explain that God loves the sinner in spite of the sin. Shortly afterward a dear friend of theirs, a civil rights worker named Jonathan Daniels, was killed by a White segregationist, Thomas Coleman. P.D. came and asked if Thomas Coleman was a bastard. Campbell replied that of course he was. Then P.D. asked if Jonathan Daniels was also. After some hesitation, Campbell replied in the affirmative. P.D. pushed it: "Which one of these two bastards do you think God loves the most?" Campbell walked to a window and looked out for a long time. Finally he turned around with tears running down his face, and said, "Damned if you ain't made a Christian out of me. And I'm not sure I can stand it" (Campbell, 1997, pp. 221-223).

I've spent a lot of time thinking about that. And the knowledge that Hitler has, at least once, looked back at me out of my own eyes, helps me to understand and appreciate it. Bishop Edmund Browning, former Presiding Bishop of the Episcopal Church, made it the goal of his twelve-year term to

Revelations on the Road

assure that in the Episcopal Church there should be no outcasts. Many were incensed at this, having their own favorite outcasts whom they believe should be left cast out where they belong. But I think Browning is right on, recognizing in this way that it truly is "all of us or none."

Roberta was a woman in her mid-forties when I was that age, whom I met when I attended a Holy Communion service at a shelter for the homeless in San Francisco. Even though I had been invited, it was clear from my appearance that I was a stranger and did not belong. Roberta met me at the door. She was painfully thin, dressed in stained and smelly clothes, with hair matted from apparent weeks of neglect. She walked with that jerky walk that one sometimes sees in persons who have been on anti-psychotic medication for a long time. Roberta welcomed me at the door, escorted me to a seat, told me not to worry because she would keep an eye out for me, and said that she would escort me to communion when the time came, which she did.

When the service was over, there was a meeting set up something like an open AA meeting, although it was not billed as such. I attended, along with my priest friend and Roberta. After each person spoke, Roberta responded. She would say, "I'm Roberta, I'm a recovering addict. You may remember I already said that." Then she would turn to the previous speaker, shift somehow in her body so that she gave the feeling of being a warm and competent therapist, and say something like, "You've been clean and sober for three weeks. Keep it up!"

Simultaneously I knew that Roberta was wounded and that I was wounded, that Roberta was Christ to others and that I was Christ to others. There was no "them" and "me," only "us." I later wrote her a note to thank her for her hospitality. I don't know if she remembered me. I do know I will never forget her.

THE GIFT OF MARGINALITY

The focus of this chapter has been on the inclusion of everyone, marginalizing no one. I would venture to guess that no one in the world, at least in today's world, has totally escaped feeling excluded at one time or another. Some of us have felt it a lot. I have learned that the feeling of strangeness, of marginality, is not simply painful; it is also a blessing, if sometimes well-disguised.

Alvin Schorr, brother of Daniel Schorr the news commentator, has been both dean of a school of social work, and a powerful bureaucrat in the Office of Economic Opportunity. He was also, even more than his brother, a rebel—from his head down to his toes. I met him when he was on the faculty where I studied for my Ph.D. I asked him once how someone so alienated by "the system" had not only survived but thrived in those two huge systems. He replied that the secret to his success and to happiness in large-scale bureaucracies had been "always to nurture and cherish a sense of marginality."

My life has been full of marginalities. After all, I am a Jew who celebrated Christmas for my first seven years. I was a kid in a small city where everyone seemed to have large families nearby, while my extended family was far away in New York City and Richmond, Virginia. I am a Christian who was born and raised as a Jew. When I was a teacher I lived twenty miles from where I taught, while most faculty lived in town. As a student I lived 100 miles from where I studied. I was a woman who taught in an almost all-male teaching environment. I was a social worker in a predominantly social science department. I am a lay person and a woman in a male-dominated, clergy-dominated church system. And I have been a liberal in several very conservative environments.

Marginality makes us aware of the pain of rejection. If we are willing, that pain can also be the wedge into the experience of others, to allow us to know their pain and to connect with them.

When I was a teenager, Rabbi Falk told our religious education class that being the Chosen People did not mean that we were better, only that we had made a deal with God to present God's truths to the rest of the world. He felt that to do that, one had to be, at least to some extent, marginalized. For God's truths had to do with justice for the marginalized, a message that must be repeated again in each generation. He ended by saying, "Perhaps in America the Jews are no longer the 'Chosen People'. We have it too easy. Perhaps in America the 'Chosen People' are Black."

So, rather than rejecting your own marginalities, cherish them as a window through which you may learn of God's compassion, and teach it to others. And remember that those you view as marginal probably have something important to give to you as well.

MAKING THE STORY YOUR OWN

◆ When in your life have you felt excluded or on the edges of things? Identify the feelings you had. Where in this experience can you find some solidarity with others who have been excluded? Choose your favorite "other," and write in her or his voice, describing the experience of exclusion.

◆ Imagine a world in which no one is excluded, like the heaven in which all are welcome. What would that be like for you? What differences would there be in your day-to-day life? What might some of the surprises be? Carry this picture into your life today, and see if you can identify places where others are excluded. How might this awareness invite you to action? to prayer?

◆ Listen to John Lennon's song, "Imagine," and compare his vision to yours.

◆ Who are the "Robertas" in your life, people whom you might have excluded, but who included you? What gifts have they given you? How might you pass them on?

FOR FURTHER READING

Brown, Christy. 1991. *My Left Foot.* Portsmouth, NH: Heinemann.
Campbell, Will. 1997. *Brother to a Dragonfly.* New York: Continuum.
Keyes, Ken. 1990. *The Handbook to Higher Consciousness.* Emeryville, CA: Publishers Group West.
Walker, Alice. 1998. *The Color Purple.* New York: Washington Square Press.

Revelation Seven: Aging As A Spiritual Journey
Aging And Letting Go

" . . . the first half of my life was filled with learning to love with abandon and the second half is filled with learning to let go"
Louise Hardin Bray (1988, 228).

Earlier we said that the goal of the spiritual journey is to live all our lives in the House of God. In our culture, many Christians of mainline churches live lives of such affluence, health, and protection, that they do not have to face the sort of letting go that really tests us and leads us to make a radical commitment to this journey. Late life gives such a test, for all of us. For even if we are blessed to have money and health and opportunities, we will have major losses. People we love will die, get sick, change, move away, and in other ways abandon us.

THE VIRULENCE OF AGISM

I believe that in our society prejudice against old age is deeper, more unconscious, and more virulent than that toward any other human characteristic: race, gender, nationality, religion, even sexual preference.

Proof? If anyone says to me, "Great job, Lynn. You did that as well as if you were a man," I will not say, "Thank you." If you say to an African-American, "Great job; you did that as well as if you were White," you will not receive any gratitude. But there is almost no one I know in our culture who, if you say, "Sixty years old! Why, I'd never have thought you to be a day over fifty," will not say, "Thank you," or at least feel a secret glee inside.

You may not find this especially surprising, but note that *this is not normal human nature!* It is a culturally conditioned response. There is a whole group of people in the Georgian region of Russia who were thought by anthropologists to be the longest lived people in the world. They were in wonderful shape, and many of them were ancient beyond our wildest expectations: 115, 135, even 160! After a number of articles appeared in *The Smithsonian* and *National Geographic* lauding their active life style, diet and attitude as the basis for their remarkable longevity, it was learned that many of these older people had lied! It was a cultural asset to be old. So even though they were only ninety or one hundred, they had lied and added years, sometimes even decades, to their ages.

Can you imagine that happening here? The only time any of us added years to our ages was when we were under the legal driving or drinking limit. That fragment of experience, however, does help us get a glimpse of a different attitude. Sometimes even in our culture a few years' life experience gives us added status and prerogatives. Wouldn't it be wonderful if we could claim that for always and ever?

Struggles and Signposts From My Life on the Road

THE GIFTS OF AGING

There are some seditious pockets of folks who appreciate, at least to some degree, the gifts of aging. Among them are Jungians. One of my friends is an Episcopal priest, psychotherapist and spiritual director. When Donna was thirty-five her nest emptied, and she went to the Jung Institute to study psychology. She felt spent, used up, useless, because her children didn't need her any more. And as she began her new career, she met what was to become one of her mentors, a woman well into her eighth decade. This woman told her, "I'm not sure you are old enough to be here. It isn't until you're past forty-five that most people are ready to become whole, and to explore the spiritual part of themselves. You're still a baby!" She was first astonished, and then felt renewed, able to take a whole new approach to life.

There are others who are able somehow to resist the culture—people who have come to see the gifts of the spiritual pilgrimage that come with long travel. For if in life we are indeed on a pilgrimage, and if that pilgrimage is designed to take us to the House of God, then the older we get, the closer we are to that place. We have wisdom to be shared!

A metaphor that describes this is hiking in the mountains. When you are on your way up, you don't know what to expect. As you follow a trail, you may find yourself climbing a long hard way up, only to be forced to turn and walk almost as far (or farther) back down again. You may wonder why the trail-maker didn't just go straight on up. You may spiral around in a circle, and find that the waterfall you walked away from turns up again a little below you on the trail. You may think you are almost there only to find that what you thought was the top is actually a false peak, and there is yet more climbing ahead.

But when you get to the top, you can stop and look around you, and see where you have come. You know then that the trail had to skirt a deep gorge, go over or around a ridge, and take all the twists and turns it did, if you were to arrive safely where you are. The view from the peak of years

Revelations on the Road

can be like that—we can find the meaning in the twists and turns, ups and downs, by looking back.

There are some sections of Hebrew and Christian scripture that bear on this topic of aging as a spiritual pilgrimage. One of my favorites is Psalm 92 where we find the words: "Those who are planted in the house of the Lord shall flourish in the courts of our God. They shall still bear fruit in old age. They shall be green and succulent." This is all for a purpose, as we hear in the last verse. It is so "that they may show how upright the Lord is, my Rock, in whom there is no fault."

We hear all our lives that our purpose is to live to the glory of God. Sometimes it just sounds like pretty words. Sometimes it evokes an ache in us, to which we do not attend. Sometimes it becomes a ravenous desire that overwhelms everything and impels us to deeper commitment. This is true no matter our age. But one of the old ones, who has lived throughout life rooted in God, shows this forth in a special way.

The members of the Yoruba tribe in Nigeria call older adults "The Wisdom People." This reflects what can happen in the life of one who does indeed live in the house of our God. Unlike the multitude of negative images of aging that assault us in the media and throughout our culture, a wisdom person is something one can aspire to become. So, let us examine the House of God as the home of the wisdom people.

In my own study of the gospel, I find many expressions of the gospel truth, and many stories that illustrate them. Each of them bears within it seeds that might be called in today's vernacular "good news and bad news." Sometimes we hear of a kingdom or realm (or house, if you will) to which we, as followers of the truth, are invited. (The *Inclusive Language New Testament* (1994) calls it the kindom; I like that, and sometimes write it "kin-dom".)

Whatever you call it, this is good news. But this kin-dom is not of this world—not such good news after all? Or think of it in terms of the pearl of great price (Mt 13:45). A pearl, valuable beyond anything else—good news!

But with a great price. Is that good news? We must admit that a pearl of great price is also bad news, for to grasp it we must let go of everything else within our reach.

The spiritual journey of aging is, like grasping that pearl, full not only of gain but of loss. This is true not only in later life, but from the moment of our conception. For in order to be born, we must leave the comfort and security of the womb. In order to go to school, we must lose the comfort and security of our all day safe haven with our mother at home. In order to marry, we must lose the comfort and security of our status as a self-determining single being. No matter what we look at as growth, as achievement, as accomplishment, as new life, it always has a shadow side of loss. Every new birth is also a death.

We see this in the imagery of baptism, where the beginning of our life in Christ is to be plunged into the waters of his death. We see it in the imagery of graduation from school where we lose the security of our friendship network to go out into the cold, cruel world. But we see it most vividly and powerfully in late life, which for many comes with a multitude of losses that can be utterly overwhelming: we may lose health, friends, spouses, employment, status, residence, and many other things that we have come to think of as making up the basic core of who we are.

And yet if we are open to the lesson, we discover that the basic core of who we are is not dependent on any of these things—material possessions, statuses, relationships, even our own bodies and our minds. It is, rather, dependent upon our being children of the kin-dom of God, residents in the House of God. And we discover this more and more if we allow ourselves to move through those losses, through the grieving of them, to be receptive to God's calling us.

Examples Of Wisdom People

I would like to tell you of a few people I know who have made that journey and have given me models for aging with grace and wisdom.

First is Aunt Marian. She was a woman who lived life with humor, zest and joy. She did not have an easy life. She married early in the twentieth century to a man who developed severe manic-depressive psychosis. Against all that she had been taught, she divorced him. It was not an easy row to hoe at that time, even harder than it is today. She raised three children alone, until her remarriage several years later. Other troubles: losing both breasts to cancer (one at age forty-five, the other at seventy-five), a heart attack, an ileostomy, the sudden loss of her most dearly beloved forty-one-year-old son-in-law to a heart attack, the hospitalization of two grandchildren with their own mental health problems. And more. With each loss, Marian grieved, hard and fast. But when she was through grieving, she was through! She rejoiced in, reveled in, delighted in life. She made Auntie Mame look like a stick-in-the-mud. Dogs loved her; children loved her; in fact the only ones who didn't love her were Olympic gold-medal sourpusses!

At my wedding reception, Aunt Marian met the bartender, and asked him, "What's the most interesting thing in your life these days?" He replied that it was his friend's new Honda. (In those days, Hondas were motorcycles, not cars.) It had all the bells and whistles possible at the time. Aunt Marian perked up her ears, confessed that she had reached the age of seventy-two without riding a motorcycle, and said she could not let one more day go by without having that experience. The last picture in my wedding album was not of Frank and me taking off for our honeymoon (that, unfortunately had come earlier), but of Aunt Marian, with her kelly green satin dress hiked up, her arms around the waist of a wonderful, long-haired young man, her white hair flying around her head, and her fingers raised in a victory sign.

Even in the last days of her life, Marian showed this zest for life. The breast cancer had metastasized to the brain, and she made a deal with her doctor to keep her at home and comfortable, but without any nasty interventions. She was very weak. But on her birthday they gave her something to pump her up a little bit and gave her a party. My father called her from 500 miles away to wish her a happy birthday, and she said, "Leon, they've given me something so I feel better. It's my birthday party, and my friends and kids and grandkids are here. I'm having a party, and I'm much too busy to be talking to you on the phone!" Thereupon she hung up on him. When the party was over, she went into a coma and she died. I could never really mourn her. I could only give thanks that I had known her and that she had provided me with a model for living and aging and dying with grace and humor and courage.

Second I will tell you about a ninety-one-year-old woman whom I interviewed for my dissertation. She lived on the second floor of a very dilapidated shack. It smelled bad, and I knew prior to the interview that she was in very poor physical and financial condition. I reluctantly walked up the steps, not wanting to be there. I left three hours later, feeling sure that I had visited in the House of God. For this woman, with failing hearing and eyesight, bad arthritis (so bad that she rarely got out), with little money and lots of pain, who had outlived both of her husbands and all nine of her children, was a woman living in the center of hope. The thing she said, that I will carry with me as long as I have my mind is, "God keeps takin' stuff away from me, and every time He does I mourns a while, and then He fills me with more of Himself!" The only way I could describe her was to say that she was marinated in God! Is there anything worth more for which to hope? She is perhaps my best example of how, in spite of loss (and, I am forced to admit, at least sometimes perhaps because of it) one can live in the House of God.

Another example was a ninety-nine-year-old woman, weighing perhaps eighty-five pounds, sitting in a wheelchair on a stage at the Kanuga Conference Center in western North Carolina during a conference on older adult ministry. She seemed to be in her own little world, and because her hearing was very poor, in a real way she was. (After hearing her speak, I later wondered if that world was really the House of God.) She came alive when someone handed her the microphone. She whipped out a small stack of three-by-five cards, and began to share with us her carefully chosen

Revelations on the Road

description of the spiritual journey of late life. Her basic message was "seize the day." She lived fully, enjoyed her life, still did volunteer work, and went to church. She said that the secret of her joy (and she was joyful beyond my powers of description) was to "find the yesses in God's nos."

Another very old woman, age ninety-six, granted me the favor of an interview. She too radiated that inner joy that I have come to see as a hallmark of residence in the House of God. I asked her to tell me what wisdom she had learned in her own aging. She said something I won't ever forget. "When I was young, I spent a lot of time kicking against the goad. I have learned to accept almost anything almost instantly." I felt cold fear, and admitted, "I'm afraid I can't even pray for that yet." "Don't worry, dear. You're not ninety-six years old!" she replied.

Finally, without telling you any of her story, let me tell you what happened when I was talking about all of this with Juanita Harris, a very wise New York City social worker, a woman in her eighties. I told her about these incidents, and she nodded wisely. I wish I could remember what she said, but I can give you a good analogy. It was as if, never having left the country, I had been telling someone about three world travelers I had met. I I imagined that one of them had come back to tell me about the University of London, the second about the Thames River, and the third about Buckingham Palace. In this imaginary conversation I would tell my listener, "I don't know where they each were, but weren't these wonderful things to see?" And I was met by a statement like, "Oh, they were all talking about London!" Juanita's words felt as if she were saying, "Oh, you are talking about the House of God!" She not only knew about it, but she had arrived there, and lived there still.

I am discovering that there are more people like these than I had ever dreamed. If we don't see them it is because we do not look for them. Even if we should see them, we do not listen long enough to hear them talk about the House of God. I can tell you without doubt that one of the major reasons that I love working with older adults is that when you do so, you are at same time working on your own spiritual pilgrimage. And the gurus and teachers, the encouragers, the pointers to the landmarks on the road to the House of God, are the wisdom people.

Monsignor Charles Fahey, a Ph.D. social worker, gerontologist and at one time head of the Third Age Center at Fordham University, has said that he believes "the future of the church is in the hands of its elders." By this he does not mean demographics (though that is also true), but rather that if our elders show by their lives and words and eyes and faces that God is their central reality, and that the church has been the institution that has nourished their faith, then the church gains credibility with young and middle aged persons as well. If on the other hand, our elders desert the church in droves, just as they withdraw from paid employment and from memberships in the Kiwanis, then the church is seen by younger persons as a club you join when you need it, but not something of significance in the overall scheme of things. So this journey is a gift received by the wisdom people, a pearl paid for at considerable cost, and one that gains value in the sharing of it with the rest of the community of faith.

The poet William Butler Yeats is one of my favorites. He tells us this very economically in four short lines in his poem "Sailing to Byzantium" (1996):

An aged man is but a paltry thing
A tattered coat upon a stick
Unless soul clap its hands and sing
And louder sing for every tatter in its mortal dress.

Teillard de Chardin, a Roman Catholic theologian, puts it most starkly perhaps as he describes this in a passage that always touches me deeply :

When the signs of age begin to mark my body (and still more when
they touch my mind); when the ill that is to diminish me or carry me
off strikes from without or is born within me; when the painful
moment comes in which I suddenly awaken to the fact that I am ill
or growing old; and above all at that last moment when I feel I am
losing hold of myself and am absolutely passive within the hands of

Revelations on the Road

the great unknown forces that have formed me; in all those dark moments, O God, grant that I may understand that it is you (provided only my faith is strong enough) who are painfully parting the fibers of my being in order to penetrate to the very marrow of my substance and bear me away within yourself (Teillard de Chardin, 1989: pp. 55-56).

And where is he being borne? To that place we have been describing, the House of God. Teillard de Chardin speaks of the end of life; but the hope that comes at the end of life is based on experiences of love transforming us now, and in experiences of God in our lives now, and in the trust in God that allows us to surrender in the way he prayed to surrender. I cannot honestly tell you that I am there yet. But I am at the point where I can pray that I will be there. And I have watched in awe as God has transformed me in other ways when I prayed honestly to be brought past obstacles to new growth. So I am coming more and more to trust that God will bring me to this total surrender by my life's end. For me that surrender opens the door to God's House. And as I see this as the most valuable of things in which to have faith, I wish it also for each of you.

MAKING THE STORY YOUR OWN

◆ What images of aging do you remember seeing as you were growing up, and since then? List some of them, and reflect on what they might mean to you about your own aging. If you had no positive images, try adding some: wisdom figure, teacher, peacemaker for example. How would this change your picture of your own old age?

◆ Think of the most important relationships you have had with older people. Take each of those people, and list the characteristics that mark them as significant for you. Can you recognize or aspire to any of these characteristics in your own life?

◆ Read over the following meditation and then close your eyes and do it. (You may want to make a tape of your own voice, talking yourself through this meditation slowly, allowing time for you to do the work between questions.)

Imagine yourself at the age of ninety-five (or, if you are close, at an age at least ten years older than you are now). Where are you living? Who are the important people in your life? What are your days like? What exciting things have you done recently or do you anticipate doing soon? What is your relationship to the church like?

Now see yourself in front of a mirror, without clothes. What do you look like? What does that mean to you?

You are now dressed again. The telephone rings. Who might it be? Why might they be calling?

Now slowly let yourself come back to the present time and place. Make some notes in your journal about what this experience was like, and any implications for your life.

◆ Try writing your own spiritual legacy for those who come after you. What have been your important revelations on the road? How might they contribute to the well-being of those who read them? (If you prefer, record them on audio or video tape.)

◆ Imagine yourself at age 120. At this wonderful old age, you find that you are like the ninety-six year old woman in that you are able to accept almost anything almost instantly. You are like the old woman, in that with whatever losses you have had, you have done your grieving and let go, and God has filled you with more of God's very self. You are aware of deep inner peace, of a kind of porousness and openness to life and others. You are a wisdom person. Let yourself sit with that for a minute, noticing what it feels like and giving thanks for it.

◆ Now from the perspective of this wisdom person, look at your present life. What can you see that would be helpful to the younger

Revelations on the Road

you? Try writing a dialogue between yourself as you are now and your 120-year-old inner wisdom person. When you are finished, what might you carry away to use in your life now and bless yourself and speed yourself on your journey?

FOR FURTHER READING

Berman, Philip and Goldman, Connie, Eds. 1992. *The Ageless Spirit.* New York: Ballantine.

Fischer, Kathleen. 1985. *Winter Grace.* New York: Paulist Press.

Guenther, Margaret.1995. *Toward Holy Ground: Spiritual Directions for the Second Half of Life.* Cambridge, MA: Cowley Press.

Harris, Maria. 1995. *Jubilee Time: Celebrating Women, Spirit, and the Advent of Age.* New York: Bantam.

Missine, Leo E. 1990. *Reflections on Aging: A Spiritual Guide.* Liguori, MO: Liguori Publications.

Raines, Robert. 1997. *A Time to Live: Seven Tasks of Creative Aging.* New York: Dutton.

Rupp, Joyce. 1988. *Praying Our Goodbyes.* Notre Dame, IN: University of Notre Dame Press.

Shalomi, Zalman Schacter and Ronald S. Miller. 1995. *From Age-ing to Sage-ing: A Profound New Vision of Growing Older.* New York: Warner Books.

Thibault, Jane. 1993. *A Deepening Love Affair: The Gift of God in Later Life.* Nashville: Upper Room Books.

Part 3:
The Mystery of Prayer

Revelation Eight: The Gift of Prayer

My best friend (other than my husband) is Clair. I used to say "was," for Clair has been dead for well over a year as I write this, but as I have continued to experience her spirit alive in my life, recently I began saying "is."

Clair is my best friend at least in part because she taught me to pray—or at least led me to want to pray, and led me to a course that taught me how. Prayer may be the most wonderful gift I have ever received, second only to life itself. I was certainly hungry for prayer. But something held me back, even after I had made a public faith commitment. And that "something" was a combination of confusion about the nature of prayer and not knowing how to pray. We'll talk about both issues here.

What Is Prayer?

One meaning of prayer is the act of asking, as in, "Pass me the salt, I pray you." While we don't currently use the word that way, when people use the word *prayer*, they often mean asking for favors for themselves or others. And much of what is problematic about prayer relates to the times when such requests are not answered.

I had a slightly broader view of prayer when I met Clair at the annual Hood Conference I mentioned earlier. Almost immediately we began talking about prayer. I confessed that in me there was a deep resistance to praying because I could think only of two reasons to pray, both of which struck me as somehow invalid at best, and at worst immensely arrogant and utterly ignorant of the nature of God.

First was, "Hot news flash; bet you didn't know *this!*" If I am praying to tell God something God does not know, and I believe God to be all-knowing, then it's at best a redundant activity. I think my prayers had been tedious for a long time because I had been dragged down by the redundancy.

A second reason, I confessed, was even worse: "I know you're God, and all that, but I have a better idea. Please do such-and-such for so-and-so." In other words, this second reason to pray was to influence God. And, who was I to correct God's plan?

Clair smiled with an impish look I was to see many times again, crossed her arms, and quietly said, "That may be true. But I continue to pray because whenever I stop praying, the coincidences stop happening." I thought about that, off and on, for over a year. What I finally was able to make of it is communicable best by analogy: if God is the electric source, prayer is plugging in. A toaster will not work unless it is plugged in to the outlet. The electricity does not leap out to make the toaster toast. And God will not take us by force. A more theological way to put it is that prayer is the place where God's grace (power) and our free will come together.

We Need To Be Taught To Pray

Somehow, during the course of that year, I made a decision that I would begin to attend more earnestly to my prayer life. But I did not know how. The Episcopal Church has a wonderful resource in the *Book of Common Prayer,* so I began to use the daily morning prayer service for individuals and families. But I often found this to be a dry and difficult exercise of the will rather than a joyous encounter with the living God, and I found myself still hungry for something more.

The next year Clair and I met again at the same conference; I told her about my difficulty. She asked if I would be interested in taking a workshop offered every year at that very conference that would teach me how to pray. It had been a tremendous help to her in her prayer life. I wanted to know more. She told me that the workshop started with everyone filling out a questionnaire about their prayer life. As I listened, I found myself increasingly and irrationally anxious. One item asked about the type of prayer we used, and I realized I didn't even know the menu.

But I did know that I wanted a deeper relationship with God, so I decided to take the workshop. Once there I learned a whole new repertoire of prayer possibilities. We spent time in silence. (Imagine prayer not as talking, but as listening!) We learned about walking and movement as forms of prayer and ways that our very breathing can be prayerful. We learned techniques of meditation. We learned about something called the prayer of the heart or the Jesus prayer, and much, much more.

That started me on a quest. I have since read and talked endlessly about prayer, tried an enormous variety of forms of prayer, and gone to innumerable workshops and retreats. I came to identify Clair as my first spiritual director and sought out others. As I learned more, I was blessed to be able to share some of it with others. Let me share, from the perspective of twenty-some years later, a little about this understanding.

Let's start with another analogy. If we compare our relationship with God to that with a beloved person, it is certainly possible to have long

Revelations on the Road

breaks in communication and still pick up where we left off. But much more often, lack of communication kills a relationship. Those with whom we have daily contact by choice are the ones we come to know and love best. When I am away from my husband, I call him daily because I *miss* him and want contact with him, just for its own sake. Certainly we are called to love God at least as much as we love our spouses.

The *Book of Common Prayer* (1979) defines prayer as "responding to God by thought and by deeds, with or without words" (p. 856). Note the word "responding." This implies that the action originates with God, and assumes all we have said in the first chapter about God's search for us being the basic source of our relationship.

This definition is pretty broad, isn't it? Well, if prayer really is the basic stuff of our communication with God, let's think again about a parallel to human relationships. If you were asked to make a comprehensive description of your communication with your spouse or children or friends, would it be sufficient never to say anything except "Would you please do X for me?" or "Would you please do X for someone else?" or "Gee, you're great!" or "Thank you," or "I'm sorry"?

In important relationships sometimes you spend time together, just hanging out. Sometimes you cry or yell; sometimes you have a pretty matter-of-fact exchange of information (e.g. "I'll be home about 6:00."). Sometimes you express love, verbally or non-verbally. Sometimes you just stare into each others' eyes. Sometimes you have a running commentary on what you're experiencing together ("Look at that red cardinal sitting on the dark green tree, whistling its song; isn't it wonderful?"). And sometimes, if the relationship is very close and is characterized by a lot of trust and ease, people just are silent together. Sometimes you aren't doing anything but being aware of the existence and presence of the other person, like the sound of a song that you might carry in the background of your consciousness from time to time.

Good news! We can have equally complex and varied exchanges with God.

Types Of Prayer

The *Book of Common Prayer* lists seven types of prayer, which I am going to rename and reorder to fit an acronym that helps in remembering them, CAPITOL. The letters standing for confession (penitence), adoration, petition, intercession, thanksgiving, oblation, and laud (praise).

The definitions, as given in the *Book of Common Prayer* (1979, pp. 856-7), are as follows:

> *Confession*: In penitence, we confess our sins and make restitution where possible, with the intention to amend our lives.
>
> *Adoration*: Adoration is the lifting up of the heart and mind to God, asking nothing but to enjoy God's presence.
>
> *Petition and Intercession*: Intercession brings before God the needs of others; in petition, we present our own needs, that God's will may be done.
>
> *Thanksgiving*: Thanksgiving is offered to God for all the blessings of this life, for our redemption, and for whatever draws us closer to God.
>
> *Oblation*: Oblation is an offering of ourselves, our lives and labors, in union with Christ, for the purposes of God.
>
> *Laud* (Praise): Why do we praise God? We praise God, not to obtain anything, but because God's Being draws praise from us.

Then one might list at least a hundred other forms of prayer: meditation and contemplation,[1] and some of the techniques to assist in them, such as breath prayer, walking prayer, sitting prayer, the use of a mandala,[2] or an icon to focus on, chanting, looking at a candle, and others. One can use a prayer journal or can contemplatively read scripture or other spiritual books, using one of a dozen methods of spiritual reading. One of the best known is the Benedictine *Lectio Divina* (divine or holy reading). One may try an

Revelations on the Road

Ignatian approach, in which one enters the Biblical narrative and becomes a part of it.

Do not be overwhelmed by the variety. What is important here is to recognize that prayer is much bigger than we allow ourselves to realize most of the time. There are so many ways to pray that it is possible, as St. Paul advises, to pray without ceasing (1 Thes 5:17). This frees us from rigidity, opens us to be teachable, and offers us a lifetime of exciting exploration.

IMAGES OF GOD ARE IMPORTANT

The way we communicate with a parent is different from the way we communicate with a spouse; both are different from the way we communicate with a small child, another driver on the road, a salesperson, or a close friend. Part of our communication pattern is based on our image of the one with whom we communicate.

This is also true with God. We will communicate very differently with the God we view as very-old-man-in-the-sky-with-a-white-beard than we will with the ground of our being. We are different with God if we view God as the clock-maker-who-set-the-whole-thing-in-motion and then took a powder—than we are if we see God as a nursing mother (Ps 131), God as lover (Hosea), or as angry judge (Mt 25:31-40). God can be seen as living water (Jn 4:10,11; 7:38), or as breath/wind/air (Jn 3:8), or as the light that is so bright that it eliminates even the need for the sun or moon (Rv 22:5). Each of these images contains a fragment of truth. Each will stretch us. We need to remember that no image of God is adequate; God is bigger than all our images.

That is part of what the second commandment, "make no graven images" is about (Ex 20:4). It is the reason for the traditional Hebraic prohibition on the use of the name YHWH—for using that name was perceived as a way of trying to control or manipulate God. Awareness that no image of God is adequate is the provocation for J. B. Phillips's marvelous little book *Your God is Too Small*; our God images must always be open to being

82

cracked or stretched. We are always called to discover new ways of seeing and understanding God. We discover that God is like many things. We discover that it is not just humankind that is made in the image of God. All of creation is also somehow made in the image of God. And yet God is beyond all our images. Thus we are called also to be iconoclasts—image breakers, snake-skin shedders, moving naked into the emerging truth into which God calls us.

REMEMBERING TO PRAY

Considering what I have said so far, it may seem surprising, but for over twenty years I have needed reminders to pray, and often still do. My longest term spiritual director was a Roman Catholic Sister of Mercy from Erie, Pennsylvania, Rita Panciera. For the first five years of our relationship, one of the most important things she did, almost every time I came to see her with yet another in an almost endless stream of spiritual dilemmas, was simply to ask ,"Have you prayed about it?" Usually I would become embarrassed, snap my fingers and say, "Uh oh!" Even after all these years, the question is still occasionally necessary; the "Uh oh!" remains embarrassing.

To follow St. Paul's advice to pray without ceasing requires years of commitment and practice, and does not happen spontaneously. One needs constant reminders. There are many ways to remind oneself to pray.

1. Setting a watch. Some years ago I bought a wonderful watch. It is not especially pretty, and is not at all feminine. What is wonderful is that it has, in addition to time and date, both an alarm and a timer. I use it for many purposes, but primarily to help in my prayer. I can set it for the amount of time I want to spend in prayer so I don't have to think about that. I can also set it to remind me to pray. I have done that when someone I care for has a big event (surgery, a job interview, etc.) happening at a particular time. I have also set it for an hour at a time during periods when I need hourly reminders to keep praying.

2. Sticky-notes are a similar gift of technology that can be used for prayer. I stick them everywhere: on the horn of my car and/or the rear view

Revelations on the Road

mirror; the mirrors in my house; my television screen, my computer screen, my refrigerator, my prayer chair, my Bible, my date book, my telephone, or even on the toilet seat. I can write on them anything that will trigger the prayer I need at the time: the name of someone for whom I want to pray, some attitude I wish to cultivate in myself, etc. (For years I wrote on many the single word: *breathe*.)

3. Define some recurring event as a trigger for prayer—the ringing of the telephone, the microwave "ping" when something is cooked, coughing when you have a cold. If there is an emotion that is causing problems, define that as a trigger to prayer and let the anger/fear/shame/ guilt/lust/ vengefulness/sadness remind you to turn to God.

4. Samples: Fr. John Hugo gave a powerful retreat for many years, one which offered a vision of the life possible for us if we truly seek to live in the House of God. He spoke of seeing all the things we covet in life as samples of God, from foods to nature to life experiences. They are samples, reminding us to "taste and see that the Lord is good" (Ps 34:8), and we can train ourselves to let them remind us of God.

The need for this never-ending stream of reminders is due to the resistance to God about which we talked earlier. Using reminders is a way for the will to cooperate with God, until the ego is tamed enough to cooperate on its own. The rebellious ego is intractable, creative and stubborn, finding new and ever more subtle ways to keep one from a true spirit of prayer, because it knows that the result of a truly prayerful life is its (the ego's) own demise.

A friend who has worked a lot with horses has said that the preferred word for "breaking" a horse is "gentling." Being gentle with oneself does not mean letting go of discipline. One just does it firmly, consistently and relentlessly, yet gently, until the work is done.

START WHERE YOU ARE

When I was a student in a master's program in social work, one of the clichés we learned was "begin where the client is." It sounds right; it sounds simple. While it is right, it is not simple! We are so preoccupied with our own agendas, our own ways of looking at things, that it is hard to *know* where the client is, and even harder to be there.

God has the same rule—and we are the client, but fortunately God is able both to know and to be where we are. That is in part what the incarnation is all about. God is anxious to meet us, constantly knocking at the door. This knowledge encourages me in the down times and relieves my fear of my own ignorance and stubbornness. I am learning that if I am willing to engage in relationship with God, and hang in there, I *will* be led.

If you too have some fear, let me reassure you. You don't have to worry about getting it right. Start where you are, and God will meet you there. If you get blocked and don't know what to do, remember Sr. Rita's question, "Have you prayed about it?" Always be open to learning more; pray for guidance. Remember that whatever you do that helps you to communicate with God, to sense God's presence and action in your life, and to give you meaning in the present and direction for the future, is prayer.

St. Teresa of Avila, who may well be the Olympic Gold Medal Champion pray-er, said that if you want to test the adequacy of your prayer, do not examine the prayer experience itself, but rather look at the result of the prayer in your life, look at "the fruit of the Spirit" (*The Interior Castle*). In the letter to the Galatians St. Paul lists what is sometimes called "the nine fold fruit of the Spirit" as "love, joy, peace, patience, kindness, goodness, faithfulness, humility and self control" (Gal 5:22). I would add thanksgiving, and you might add your own indicators—for example hope, generosity, or authenticity. All are manifestations of growth in God's Spirit.

The interesting thing about this is that it is also very practical. You can tell if you are more loving, joyful, peaceful, patient, or kind. You can tell if your self-control is growing or ebbing. The fruit of the spirit is totally incompatible with a "me first, last and always" position, which is the basic position of the ego. So the rule I use is:

If the fruit of the Spirit is growing in you, keep on praying as you are. If the fruit of the Spirit is not growing in you, experiment with other ways to pray, (and pray for guidance).

I will end this chapter with a postscript about coincidence. The second year at the Hood Conference I went running up to Clair and said, "You have changed my life!" She gave me the look one has when thinking, "Who *is* this person?" After we each got over our embarrassment, we picked up our conversation again. I reminded her of what she had said about coincidence, and told her what it had meant for me. We both gave thanks for the work God had done in my life. Clair tried to give God all the credit, but I wouldn't let her. "It may be that God used you as an instrument, and I too believe that to be the case, but *you had to say your 'yes.'* And you *were* the instrument God used, so you might as well just say, 'You're welcome.'" She smiled and said, "You're welcome."

Coincidence dogged our relationship from then on, making point after point. The last evening of that conference I was telling a visitor in my room about the original incident, and, for the first time during the entire conference, Clair walked into my room, just as I was quoting her statement: "Whenever I stop praying, the coincidences stop happening."

The most remarkable coincidence with Clair came the winter after our third Hood Conference. Between the other Hood conferences we had had no contact. During the first three I had roomed with a friend from Erie, my home town. When I got the publicity for the fourth Hood Conference I thought of asking Clair to be my roommate the following summer. I decided to write rather than call, to give her time to think about it, and to come up with a tactful way to say "no" if she had other plans. That evening, long before my letter reached her, Clair called to ask me to be her roommate. The gift of that coincidence! The utter gratuitousness of it! And the message went deep, deep, deep into my heart. I realized what prayer was about in a new way: not seeking to manipulate events in my favor or that of another; not even primarily seeking a way to send a message to God. Prayer is about developing a relationship of love with God so that you are united in heart, even more than I am with Clair; even more than I am with my husband; perhaps even more than I am with myself. Abraham Heschel says it starkly: "Indeed, to pray does not only mean to seek *help;* it also means to seek God.".

MAKING THE STORY YOUR OWN

◆ Who or what is your "Clair"—someone or something that helped you to make an initial commitment to the prayer journey? Reflect on the gift this has been to you, and be thankful.

◆ If a coincidence is a miracle in which God wishes to remain anonymous, think about where God has been active in your life that you haven't noticed before. What does this mean to you?

◆ Write your own definition of prayer. Look again at the definition of prayer from the Book of Common Prayer (found on page 80). Look at my definition of prayer ("prayer is the place . . . " found on page 78). Look at Heschel's statement at the end of this chapter. How do these other definitions of prayer compare with yours?

◆ Frederick Buechner has a wonderful little book called *The Alphabet of Grace*, in which he finds things beginning with each letter of the alphabet for which to give thanks. Building on his idea, take a clean sheet of paper. At the left margin write the alphabet, one letter on each line. Try making a list under each letter of ten things for which you are thankful.

When you are through, go back through your list, and sit with each thing for a while, remembering the context of the gift and anything else about it that you can. Who else was involved? What surprises were there in the gift? What did you learn? Give thanks to God for each gift.

You may want to make this a long term project, for you could spend a lot of time on it, and you may want to do it thoroughly and

Revelations on the Road

at a leisurely pace. You could take a letter a day or even a letter a week. Let this develop in you the habit of looking for the gift in things and of being thankful. (Perhaps gratitude itself is a gift.)

For Further Reading

Bloom, Anthony. 1988. *Beginning to Pray*. New York: Paulist Press.

Brooke, Avery. 1986. *Hidden in Plain Sight: The Practice of Christian Meditation*. Nashville, TN: The Upper Room.

Foster, Richard. 1992. *Prayer: Finding the Heart's True Home*. San Francisco: HarperSanFrancisco.

Green, Thomas, SJ. 1977. *Opening to God*. Notre Dame, IN: Ave Maria Press.

_____. 1995. *When the Well Runs Dry*. Notre Dame, IN: Ave Maria Press.

Keating, Thomas. 1995. *Open Mind, Open Heart: The Contemplative Dimension of the Gospel*. New York: Continuum Press.

Kelley, Thomas. 1996. *A Testament of Devotion*. San Francisco: HarperSanFrancisco.

Kelsey, Morton. 1997. *The Other Side of Silence*. New York: Paulist Press.

Lindberg, Anne Morrow. 1975. *Gift From the Sea*. New York: Pantheon.

McFague, Sallie. 1987. *Models of God: Theology for an Ecological Nuclear Age*. Minneapolis: Fortress Press.

Pennington, M. Basil. 1987. *Centering Prayer*. Garden City, NY: Image.

_____. 1998. *Lectio Divina: Renewing the Ancient Practice of Praying the Scriptures*. NY: Crossroad Publications.

Progoff, Ira. 1992. *At a Journal Workshop*. New York: Tarcher.

St. Teresa of Avila. 1972. *Interior Castle*. Garden City, New York: Image.

Thompson, Marjorie. 1995. *Soul Feast: An Invitation to the Christian Spiritual Life*. Louisville, KY: Westminster John Knox Press.

Wiederkehr, Macrina 1988. *A Tree Full of Angels: Seeing the Holy in the Ordinary*. San Francisco: Harper Collins.

Revelation Nine: Teach Me What I Need to Know

Frank and I were on our way back to Pennsylvania from Colorado in 1986 in our seventeen-year-old pop-up tent camper, driving at breakneck speed to get through the wilderness of Illinois, when we were stopped short by a broken leaf spring in the trailer suspension. If you don't know what a leaf spring is, you are no less knowledgeable than I was, but having one break is a good way to learn what one is. A leaf spring is a spring composed of several overlapping layers (leaves) that form a flat U-shape and hold the body of your vehicle up off the axle. This is desirable, because if it sits directly on the axle, it shreds the tire as it rotates. You do *not* want to proceed with a broken leaf spring.

Revelations on the Road

So we found ourselves on the shoulder of I-80 near Joliet, in a dilemma. We did not want to leave the trailer because it held much of what we valued of our worldly goods. We did not want to leave me with the trailer because I might not fare much better than the trailer left alone. (Worse than picking up a hitchhiker is becoming an involuntary one.) That left me as "scout"—a role I cherished only slightly less than involuntary hitchhiker. For it involved driving Frank's truck, with a clutch that did not engage until you had your left knee near your left ear, and a wheel that did not turn the truck until you had rotated it about 270 degrees, at which time it acted in what I perceived to be a precipitous manner.

Furthermore there was the issue of what I would be scouting—those men who smile broadly and say things like, "Aha, little lady. You have a broken leaf spring. Well don't you worry your pretty little head about it. I'll fix it for you at the bargain price of seven thousand three hundred and two dollars and seven cents . . . a week from next Friday." But I set off, trying my usually effective cheerer-upper, "I'm having an adventure." When that didn't work, and I recognized a rather unmanageable pile of anxiety sitting like a huge boulder on the floor of my stomach, I turned to God and said, "I don't know why I'm so scared, but I am. So there must be something here for me to learn. I'll pay attention, and You teach me what I need to know."

That helped, for I found myself paying attention very closely to everything that was happening, looking for the lessons and teachings, and amazingly not feeling the anxiety any more. The first exit from the interstate was another interstate going to Florida, and the teaching was clear, "skip that one." The second exit beckoned, and I got off, passing a long, low, red brick, windowless building. I noticed a gas station and headed for it, only to find out that the only employee there didn't know what a leaf spring was either. But she sent me to the next door neighbor, "a nice man who knows a lot about cars." At that point I found the anxiety coming back, but I decided to follow instructions. I knocked on the next-door neighbor's door.

A tall man in a tee shirt appeared. He listened to my tale of woe and, as I talked, developed a twinkle in his eye. When I paused for a moment, he said, "Whoa. Did you see that low red brick building as you exited the highway?" I said that I had (remember, I was paying attention). He smiled the biggest smile I had ever seen and said, "Well, that's the Joliet Spring Company. They *make* leaf springs, from scratch, for everything from kids' toys to eighteen wheelers. And there are only seven places like them in the country!" Three hours later, having been taught how to move a vehicle without a leaf spring (put a block of wood between the axle and the body of the vehicle), and having had a laughter-filled meal at a handy nearby Bob Evans Restaurant, we were on our way. After I stopped jumping up and down and clicking my heels together in glee, I stopped to thank God and to reflect on what I had been taught.

The Learning: Ask, "Teach Me What I Need To Know"

The answer came immediately. "Whatever happens, always pray 'teach me what I need to know,' and I *will* teach you. I will not promise that the lesson will always be as flashy as this, or as much fun, but if you ask the question, trusting me, *and* pay attention, I *will* teach you."

I cannot say that I have never been anxious since. I cannot even say that whenever I felt anxiety I used it wisely to turn me to the prayer "teach me what I need to know." But it happens often enough, and in the times where the not-knowing seems important enough, that I look back on the broken leaf spring as a sacrament—"an outward and visible sign of an inward and spiritual grace" as defined in the *Book of Common Prayer* (p. 857). This experience has deeply changed me. Now decisions that I know will affect my future are made not only with the use of my intellect, but prayerfully, trusting that God will teach me what I need to know.

One Step Enough For Me

At one of my times of decision making, I read the words of a hymn by Cardinal John Henry Newman, "Lead Kindly Light," which have since become very important to me and which essentially offer the same prayer as "teach me what I need to know." The first verse prays:

Lead, kindly Light, amid the encircling gloom,
*   Lead thou me on;*
The night is dark, and I am far from home;
*   Lead thou me on;*
Keep thou my feet; I do not ask to see
The distant scene; one step enough for me.

I found myself identifying with Newman, especially when I read the second verse:

I was not ever thus, nor prayed that thou
*   Shouldst lead me on;*
I loved to choose and see my path; but now
*   Lead thou me on.*
I loved the garish day, and, spite of fears,
Pride ruled my will: remember not past years.

And the third and final verse provides a view of the trust we come to as God, step by step, deepens our faith:

So long thy power hath blest me, sure it still
*   Will lead me on*
O'er moor and fen, o'er crag and torrent till
*   The night is gone;*
And with the morn those angel faces smile
Which I have loved long since and lost awhile.
(Hymn 430. Church Pension Fund, 1940)

I have learned that this wisdom applies both to the big picture (my whole life) and to the small picture of specific projects on which I work. As an example, let me describe how this worked in writing this book. The book started with a gift of God—the idea coming during the review of my journals. I wrote:

It is amazing how it seems the longer I stay on the spiritual pilgrim-
age, the more times I find these little gems of experience that seem

*to give me guidance for the rest of the road. And what a wonderful
coincidence that the things that come to me seem to be helpful to
others when I share them. Paul talks about the gifts being given not
for the recipient but for the whole body (1 Cor 12), but when I can
see that over and over in my own life it is an amazing encouragement! It might not be as dramatic as Paul's revelation on the road,
but it is mine. Hey! How about that as a theme for a book?*

This same process was the inspirational flash for my dissertation:
*Connections: the Place of the Church in the Personal Networks of the
Elderly.* And it happens over and over in things ranging from what I do in my
work with the church, to thinking of Christmas presents to get people, and in
many many other ways.

DISCERNING GOD'S VOICE

When I have talked with others about the experience of prayer and
asking God, "Teach me what I need to know," I often am asked how one
knows when the voice is of God and when it is some other voice. Making
this distinction is called discernment; it requires prayer and patience. It is
easy to fool oneself, and one can never be absolutely sure one is correct,
but one can become clearer and clearer. The trick is to listen. You learn to
know your mother's voice, and to distinguish it from other voices by listening
attentively. Jesus says, "My sheep know my voice" (Jn 10:4).

Let us look at a few ways to hear God's voice. First, sometimes God
speaks through our own heart. Psalm 16 includes the remarkable verse:

*I bless the Lord who gives me counsel;
In the night also my heart instructs me.*

To help us understand this, it is useful to know that the verses of the
Psalms, set up as couplets, are often designed to repeat the same thought
in two different ways, helping us to deepen our understanding of what is
meant. Thus we can see this verse as saying that one of the ways God

gives counsel is from our own hearts. I am told that a great saint once said that God guides us through the deepest desires of our own hearts.

Knowledge of our deepest desires comes in a number of ways. It can come in prayer, in reading scripture, in listening to a sermon, in hearing someone else's story, in watching a movie. It can come from our dreams. It can come in spiritual direction or psychotherapy, or in receiving the counsel of a good friend. We recognize it when something deep inside shouts, "Yes" or whispers, "Pay attention!" However it comes, it is important to learn to follow our own deepest wisdom, trusting that it does indeed come from God.

Second, we come to know God's voice by learning more about God's nature. This happens not only in prayer, but in reading scripture (the record of God's action in human history) and the writings of others we know to be ahead of us on the road. The more we learn, the easier it is, at least at times, to say, "That is not in keeping with God's nature."

When my brother was about four he did something that absolutely infuriated my mother. She blew up at him, and in a totally uncharacteristic way threatened to tie him up, wrap him in a box, and send him back to Macys. He looked at her, totally unconcerned, and replied innocently, "You wouldn't do that, Mommy. You love me too much!" This family story came to me as I began writing about discerning God's voice. My brother had come to know my mother's character so well, that he knew her authentic voice even when she did not! This couldn't happen with God, but it was a good teaching that as we come to know God better, we know what God will and won't do, which helps us discern what God wants of us.

St. Ignatius is perhaps the greatest expert of all time on discernment of God's will. He suggests that when we are considering a choice between two courses of action, we first make sure that what we are thinking of doing is not sinful. (Sin is never in keeping with God's will for us.) Next we should subject it to the rational power of our mind by such methods as making lists of the positive and negative consequences of each choice. Sometimes this is sufficient to make clear what our decision ought to be. If not, we turn to the process of discernment. Here we examine what Ignatius calls the "desolations" and "consolations."

For the person who is committed to doing God's will in all things, Ignatius says the Holy Spirit will work in consolations (such as peace of mind, courage, joy, zeal, patience and simplicity), leading to an increase in spiritual progress and increased vitality of faith, hope and love. On the other hand, the evil one works through desolations (agitation, apathy, inner impatience with God, dejection with a focus on the self, etc.) in order to increase susceptibility to temptation and diminish the vitality of one's faith, hope and love. (For more on this, see the section on rules for discernment of spirits in any good translation of the *Spiritual Exercises of St. Ignatius.* A contemporary work on Ignatian discernment, one which I find very useful, is Thomas Green's *Weeds Among the Wheat.*)

Another way to think about discernment has to do with the tension between love and fear. I believe that the opposite of love is not hate, which was what I thought it was when I was a child; nor is it indifference, which is what I thought as a socially-concerned young woman. It is fear. I have been unable to find a single instance where, when I felt called to a loving act and did not follow through on the call, the hesitation was not out of fear. The fear may be subtle and difficult to identify. It may be as terrifying as the fear of personal annihilation if I let go of behaviors that have felt like core self to me. Or it may be as simple as the fear that I do not have enough time. But there is always fear. Just as "perfect love casts out fear" (1 Jn 4:18), perfect fear does a pretty good job on love, too.

A friend once attended a conference at which Madeleine L'Engle spoke and came back all excited with one idea: L'Engle had said that whenever an angel appears in scripture, the message is accompanied by the admonition "fear not." Mary's call to be the mother of God is certainly a prime example.

The angel Gabriel . . . came to (Mary) and said, "Greeting, favored one! The Lord is with you. " But she was much perplexed by his words and pondered what sort of greeting this might be. The angel said to her, "Do not be afraid, Mary, for you have found favor with God" (Lk 1:26-30).

In calling Joshua to take on the leadership of the Hebrew people after Moses' death, several times God sends the message, "Be strong and of good courage," first through Moses, and then directly. (See Deuteronomy 31 and Joshua 1.) A friend has done a scripture study of the subject and informs me that the commandment not to fear comes over 350 times in the Bible! Anthony de Mello, in a taped conference called "Wake Up to Life," made this same point. Being aware, which might equally well be called enlightenment, or walking in faith, makes one unafraid.

You can take the fear, assume (in Ignatius's terms) that it is not of God, resist it, remain faithful to your commitments, remain faithful in prayer, and wait patiently for the signs that give you the encouragement to proceed. Wait for the "kindly light."

MAKING THE STORY YOUR OWN

◆ Take a clean sheet of paper and turn it sideways. Draw a line across the middle of the page. Put the date of your birth at one end of the line and, if you wish, the estimated date of your death at the other. (If you prefer, leave the other end undated.) Mark the significant events of your life on the line, particularly those which have resulted in new directions or important new learning for you. Above the line, write a short description of each event. Below the line write a short, terse description of the learning in the event, such as "teach me what I need to know."

When you are finished, you may wish to take each of these learnings and do some thinking or writing about them. This could become a project for a sustained effort, such as during Lent one year, or on a retreat. Cherish the learnings, and give thanks for them. Ask God to keep offering you opportunities to learn. These are your own revelations on the road.

The Mystery of Prayer

◆ Think of times when you are sure that God was leading you. Identify the characteristics for you of that leading. God leads each of us uniquely. St. Ignatius described for his followers the way he had found to discern God's voice: the desolations and consolations. This came out of the experience of his own life. If, based on your own unique experience of God, you were going to teach your followers how to discover God's voice among all the competing voices clamoring for their attention, how would you guide them?

FOR FURTHER READING

Farnham, Suzanne G. et. al. 1991. *Listening Hearts: Discerning Call in Community*. Harrisburg, PA: Morehouse.

Green, Thomas J., S.J. 1984. *Weeds Among the Wheat*. Notre Dame, IN: Ave Maria Press.

Ignatius of Loyola. 1997. *The Spiritual Exercises of St. Ignatius.* Translated by Pierre Wolff. Garden City, N. Y.: Image.

Revelation Ten: Be Here Now
(Time As A Spiritual Issue)

    I have been fascinated by time as long as I can remember, although initially I did not see it as a spiritual issue. One of the experiences that shaped my thinking about time happened when I was in my senior year of college. I was in a stall in a dormitory bathroom when two other college women entered, talking as if they were alone. One said to the other, "It is November now. I want to meet him before the Holidays, be engaged in February, and be married in June."

    I was horrified, in part because the goal of marriage was so far from the mind of what I liked to think of as the "typical Barnard student." But the worst thing about this was that in spite of whatever she thought she was saying, in front of me loomed the rest of her life. She would wait to meet "him," wait to get engaged, wait to be married, wait to have her children, wait for them to go to school, wait for her husband to retire and then I guess wait for him or for herself to die. When would she actually start to live?

I decided at that very moment that whatever she did, I was going to start to live right then! No more was school going to be a preparation for life. It would be life itself. As a teenager I had heard my mother respond over and over again to my impatient moanings, "I can't wait for such and such to happen" with a pat phrase that came to life only as I finally understood it: "Don't wish your life away." I learned it that day in the Barnard dorm lavatory, and I have been continuing to learn it ever since.

In Greek there are two words for time: *kairos* and *chronos*. *Kairos* refers to those almost time-less moments that seem to be eternal, moments that create a change so profound that nothing is ever afterward the same. *Chronos* is time as measured by the clock. While I did not have the vocabulary at that time, what I decided was to seek *kairos* rather than worrying so much about the passage of *chronos*.

I believe that the issue of our relationship to time is at the heart of our spiritual malaise as a society. One comparison helps me comprehend this. We tend to see time as a scarce commodity. It is reflected clearly in the language we use about time: we save it, spend it, use it. Another way of living, more in kairos, is to view time as an environment that sometimes gets polluted and in which we "live and move and have our being" (Acts 17:28).

Our relationship to time is virtually addictive. In this chapter I will tell you something of my own experience of time-addiction, and then expand the focus to look at how this is true for so many of us in today's world. Finally we'll look at some ways of finding a healthier rhythm.

Psychologists say that major patterns in our lives are what they call *over-determined*. They do not happen simply as a result of one causal event; they happen because dozens and dozens of things seem to conspire in order for them to happen. My relationship to time was certainly over-determined. First, my mother is the world's greatest planner. If she takes a big trip, her luggage is packed a month ahead of time. Living in a household run with this lavish attention to detail and to advance planning pushed me to be very conscious of time.

Second, my primary affirmation in life came from the recognition of achievement, of being known for getting things done. This was true at home, at school, among my friends, at the Temple, and in every aspect of my life. The highest praise from Mother was to hear at the dinner table "Lynn got a lot accomplished today." And as time went on, others took up the song, "I don't know how you get so much done!" and, "I hate to even ask you this, because you're so busy, but would you . . . ?" Getting as much done in as little time as was humanly possible became an all-pervasive, if largely unconscious goal in my life.

Third, being busy was a way of avoiding the void. I think this is true for all of us. One of the primary characteristics of our era is busy-ness. I believe it has come to be a status symbol. If someone asks, "How are you?" and you don't reply, "Fine, but terribly busy." there is something wrong with you. Busy-ness is evidence of our importance. The fact that we can become so busy that there is nothing of substance left underneath does not seem to enter our consciousness. In fact we are so busy we don't have time to let much of anything really enter our consciousness at all. Another way to put this is that the drug of choice in twenty-first century North America is adrenaline.

The destructive side of busy-ness is increasingly being recognized today. Harry Chapin's 1960s song "Cat's in the Cradle" is a popular expression of the intergenerational pattern: father's sin passed on to son, not as sin but as a positive identity. In case you don't know the song, it begins with several verses in each of which a boy asks his dad to do things with him. The father responds each time with a litany of things he has to do, but promises one day they will have time together, and says, "we'll have a good time then." The son replies that it's okay, and expresses his love, "I'm gonna be just like you." The last verse is sung by the father, now an older man, asking his son to spend some time with him. The son recites his own litany of busy-ness, and the father ends up musing, "And as I hung up the phone it occurred to me—he'd grown up just like me."

Ann Wilson Schaef has a book called *Meditations for Women Who Do Too Much*. Gerald May discusses the theme of busy-ness as addiction in his books *Addiction and Grace* and *The Awakened Heart*. Many others address this today and look at it as a spiritual issue. I believe the irresistible combination of family programming, organizational rewards for productivity, social recognition and our innate fear of the void make for a very deeply programmed, very destructive pattern in the lives of many, if not most, postmodern Western women and men.

In reading the journals I wrote from my 30s through my 50s, I notice a constant background pattern of anxiety attributed to perceived time pressure. Over and over I listed all the things that had to be done, expressing surety that they could not be done in the time before the arrival of whatever deadline the world or I had set for them arrived. Even things that are enjoyable have the juice squeezed out of them by this kind of interior pressure.

And when I finished the list, did I rest? No, I did something unconsciously that I now call "upleveling priority three to priority one when priorities one and two are finished." If nothing else, there is always a pile (usually several) of unread things that I neither throw away nor read. If there is nothing else I "have to" do, I can define reading those piles as a "have to" task. That simple redefinition is sufficient to keep me feeling guilty and anxious. The phrasing of the task is important: "I have to" do x or y or z. (How else to keep up the pressure?) If I said, "Wow, look what I get to do next," it might not feel like work! Or I might decide I'll "get to" do it tomorrow.

This pattern is so deeply ingrained that changing it takes years of work, lots of imaginative ways to raise awareness, and lots of new tools to undo old patterns. I would share some of those that have worked, to one degree or another, for me, as I am fully convinced that this issue is one widely

The Mystery of Prayer

shared by most middle class Americans today. And those involved in the church, rather than being exempt from it, are among the worst offenders/victims. (We all are both.)

The first tool is keeping in mind that now is "real" time. Just as the student in school defined the moment in which she was living as "waiting" rather than "living", we are capable of finding other ways to exclude the present moment from real time. If someone said, "Do you really want to spend your life in such a harried way?" I would reply, "Oh, I won't spend my life this way. I'm just busy until _____." I could fill in the blank with any number of good causes. Until the dissertation is completed. Until our accreditation process is finished. Until we get ready to move. Until we get the school for spiritual direction up and running. Until . . . but like tomorrow, "until" never comes. If I really choose to change the pattern, I must start now. I call the state of mind in which I make an exception for this minute "transitional time"—this is the time I choose not to live in the moment, but only "until." The slogan that can help me to get out of this state of mind is "all time is real time."

The emphasis on the now is one which comes from many spiritual teachers. Ram Dass has been one of mine. He was once Richard Alpert, a Jewish psychologist at Harvard, contemporary with his better known colleague Timothy Leary. They began a quest for greater consciousness with the help of psychedelic drugs. After Alpert was tossed out of Harvard, he went to India. There he decided that spirituality, rather than drugs, was a better path to his goal. I have heard him in person, and have read several of his books, the best known of which has a title that expresses his main message (and my hoped-for relationship with time): be here now. It seems terribly obvious: where else could one be? But we spend much of our time, spiritually and psychologically, anywhere but here now.

I heard Ram Dass speak once about this issue. He talked about the quest for being high that keeps one from enjoying even the high of the present moment. He said something like this: "Many of you are experts at

103

Revelations on the Road

getting high. You just don't know how to stay high. That is why you are here. In the middle of a nice dinner, you are wondering about the dessert; in the middle of the dessert you are thinking about kissing her. While you are kissing her, you wonder about what's next. And in the middle of making love, you wonder what's in the refrigerator."

We are insatiably committed to the quest for more: more things, more experiences, more honors, more knowledge. If the focus is on the "more," we never enjoy what we actually have. Ram Dass has a wonderful image. He says that we are born on a clock face at 12:00. We live one go-round of the hand to 12:00 again. From 12:00 to 6:00 we are taking on-possessions, degrees, loved ones, relationships, statuses, connections, and all manner of things designed to buttress our sense of who we are and to make our life easy and pleasant. From 6:00 until 12:00 we are letting go, sometimes voluntarily and sometimes not. When we get to 11:59 all we have left is enough body and ego to be of service. This is where I believe Jesus was, and where Ram Dass says the Buddha was, and where it looks to me Gandhi was.

If you talk to someone before 6:00 about letting go they think you hate life, hate yourself, and are sick. Who would stop eating, having sex, watching TV, or buying and having and using the good things of life? It is weird, because if someone makes that sacrifice for a more earthly goal—for example to train for the Olympics—we admire them and write them up in the news media and heap praise on them. But if one does such things for the purpose of glorifying God, or to move toward holiness, we view them through a different lens indeed. They are kooks or weirdos. Barry Goldwater said something in his 1964 campaign for president with which I did not agree: that extremism in defense of liberty was not a sin. But I might paraphrase him that extremism in pursuit of holiness might be an interesting antidote to the culture of our times.

In regard to the clock face, I have many selves. You probably do too. And they may be located at different places on the clock. We may have parts of us at 1:00 and parts of us at 6:00 and parts at 11:59.9. From the few

The Mystery of Prayer

things I have been able to let go of, I can tell you that rather than feeling like self-punishment, it is like dropping rocks from my backpack to speed me on my way.

One way to describe this is to write the word now as follows:

n O w

Cover up the "w." The word represents what life tells us if we try to live in the past, clinging to what no longer is: "NO!"

Now cover up the "n." The word is now telling us what happens when we try to squeeze our consciousness out of the present and into the future: "OW!"

But if we learn to live as Ram Dass teaches, being truly here now, we can cover up both the "n" and the "w" and hear the wonder of our own healthy, loving, self saying in wonder "Oh!" It is only here now that we can be fully alive, and being here now is so wonderful that we cry "Oh!" when we are.

If it were easy to do, everyone would do it. It is, in many ways, simple; but it is not easy. After working at it for years, I once wrote in my journal:

It is so easy to slip out of Your Presence and into transitional time. It requires constant, continual vigilance, prayer, and attention to stay with You. Even then it takes Grace to will it and Grace to do it, and partnership with You that makes it possible.

Twelve step programs recognize this. One of their slogans is "One day at a time." I have friends in AA and Alanon who tell me it is really more like one hour at a time, or even one minute at a time. This is true when we are in pain, but it is also the secret to truly being alive even when we are not in pain.

One year in Lent I spent twenty minutes per day meditating using a mandala: a circular figure on which one focuses the eyes. A mandala is usually filled with symmetrical symbols, but one does not use it to think consciously

105

Revelations on the Road

about the symbolism; you just let your eyes see and your conscious mind rest. The symbol I used was a facsimile of a cross drawn with a magic marker in a book entitled *Living Simply Through the Day* (a whole book teaching how to be here now) by Tilden Edwards. It looked something like this:

Figure 1. The Cross

    I found that as I kept my eyes on it, it began to transform into other shapes: sometimes the horizontal line would become very thin and the vertical become very wide. Once when that had happened, I reflected afterward

The Mystery of Prayer

on the symbolic meaning of the experience. The center of the cross seemed to represent the point where time intersects eternity. If one is fully in the moment, it opens up and we find ourselves in eternity. This is another way of seeing the "Oh!"

Ken Keyes is, like Ram Dass, a student both of psychology and of Eastern religion. He has written a little book entitled *The Handbook to Higher Consciousness,* which is a "how to" book for busy westerners wanting to learn to be here now. I must confess some discomfort at recommending it because it is a very hard sell on itself. On almost every page there is something that sounded to me like "If you do everything I say, your life will be perfect." But I have come to believe that it is true. It is also truly simple—just not easy. If you let go of expectations, your life will be perfect; you will be living in the House of God.

Ken Keyes gives some helpful ways of keeping the goal in mind. He defines all things I believe I must have in order to be happy as addictions (other than air, water, a minimal amount of food, and such like). If I insist on having them, I will be unhappy when I don't. If I can "uplevel my addictions to preferences," I can choose to be happy even when I do not have them. Keyes gives help through such techniques as reframing. For example, I can define my pain as an opportunity for growth and use it as such. I can remind myself constantly that I have everything I need to be happy.

When having a problem with another person, Keyes recommends I use my imagination to get inside the other person's skin, to try to understand why the one who is a problem to me is behaving that way. Then if all else fails, define that person as my teacher, put there by the Universe as a gift I need to help me on my journey. Keyes presents life in such a way that there is no escape hatch to call something transitional—it is all real time."

Another way we hear this lesson framed is in the advice to bloom where you are planted. We can even find it in the Bible. Jeremiah in addressing the Hebrews in exile, says; "Seek the peace of the city whither I have caused you to be carried away captives; and pray to the Lord for it; for in the peace thereof shall you have peace" (Jer 29:7).

Revelations on the Road

Psalm 131 is even more explicitly descriptive of this way of being.

O Lord, I am not proud,
I have no haughty looks.
I do not occupy myself with great matters
Or with things that are too hard for me.
But I still my soul and make it quiet,
Like a child upon its mother's breast;
My soul is quieted within me .

THE ONE THING NECESSARY

I had an experience in Lent of 1988 that helped me get a handle on this issue. I was co-mentoring an Education for Ministry (EFM)[1] group in Sewanee, Tennessee. For each of the six weeks of Lent we happened, by coincidence, to deal with the issue of being too busy. Part of the EFM group process is called theological reflection, and it involves first exploring an issue in the life of one of the group members, and then looking at a relevant part of the tradition, often from scripture. Each week we looked at a different passage.

During Lent that year I had been consciously praying to have the addictive attachment to time removed from me. I was clear by that time that the process was addictive, and realized from what I knew of twelve step programs that I needed help and could not do this work on my own. So I prayed. But I felt like someone locked deep in a prison with heavy walls and doors, knocking for someone to let her out, and having no sense that anyone could even hear, much less that anyone would come to help.

My husband gave me a book during that season, entitled *The Painted Bird* by Jersy Kosinski. It was a fascinating and deeply troubling autobiographical novel about a Jewish youth in Eastern Europe, given by his parents to a peasant family in order to save his life. Viewed with suspicion, he became the village scapegoat. At one point he witnessed the gang rape of a girl, and in making his escape was followed by the perpetrators. He found

The Mystery of Prayer

himself near a barrel that somehow had become full of rats, their claws making rasping noises against the side of the barrel as they desperately tried to get out. In their frenzy, they were shredding and cannibalizing each other. The leader of the perpetrators fell into the barrel and was devoured.

The image stayed with me for a long time, like a ghastly nightmare. Finally I recognized it: the image of rats in a barrel perfectly fit the feeling of anxiety in my stomach when I began the "have to do this, have to do that" routine on myself. But I felt no joy in the recognition, only more deeply trapped.

Our EFM group met on Monday mornings. We met the day after Easter and someone asked, "How are you?" Instead of responding with a litany of how busy I was, I replied, to my astonishment, "I'm great!" I realized at that moment that, without my even noticing that it had happened, on Easter Day my prayer had been answered! I felt totally at peace, totally spacious and expansive, totally present and unrushed, totally grateful and joyful. And until asked, I hadn't even noticed that my prayer had been answered. I hadn't realized it until I heard my own answer!

Again that day we dealt with busy-ness. The scripture we picked made us all laugh because it was the only section of scripture any of us could think of that really addressed this problem, and only after six weeks of dealing with the issue, had we finally thought of it. Have a read:

> (Jesus) entered a certain village where a woman named Martha welcomed him into her home. She had a sister named Mary, who sat at the Lord's feet and listened to what he was saying. But Martha was distracted by her many tasks; so she came to him and asked, "Lord, do you not care that my sister has left me to do all the work by myself? Tell her then to help me." But the Lord answered her, "Martha, Martha, you are worried and distracted by many things; there is need of only one thing. Mary has chosen the better part (Lk 10:38-42).

My colleague, who was leading the discussion that day, then asked what has become for me one of the most important questions there is: "In your life, what is the one thing necessary?" And I *knew!* The knowing came in a flash; it was totally clear. In my life, the one thing necessary is to know, deep in my gut and heart, beyond the shadow of a doubt, that God loves me. When I know this, all work becomes a way of saying, "thank you," and is done in relaxed and joyful ease, rather than in the frenzied fear that somehow there will not be enough time, that something essential will not get done, and that I will somehow be punished.

I recovered a memory at that time that seemed to be connected to the familial roots of my fear. It happened when I was about eight or nine years old. My mother's birthday is in mid-May, and sometimes falls on Mother's Day. It did that year. Wanting to please her, I got up early so I could take breakfast to her in bed. I cooked everything, found a wicker tray with side pockets, put in a napkin, and was preparing to take the tray upstairs. I was feeling proud, for the tray was decorated with a flower and a doily. The coffee was hot, the orange juice cold, and everything looked like something Martha Stewart might make.

But before I could carry the tray upstairs my mother quietly came down and walked into the kitchen. She glanced past the tray, not even seeing it, and looked around in horror, exclaiming "Oh my God, will you look at the mess in this kitchen! Who will ever clean it up?"

I do not remember what happened next. I only know that somehow my own shame, disappointment and hurt translated into the subsequent need to try to do everything perfectly, and more important, to cover all possible bases. I carried a fear that something (probably something I didn't even notice, and therefore couldn't prevent) would happen and someone important would see what I have come to call "the mess in the kitchen."[2] What happened on that Easter Monday was a healing of the pain, and a liberation from the power of the memory. Along with this miracle came a new understanding: I can never do enough to earn God's love, but, thank God, I do not have to. God sees the tray and overlooks the "mess in the kitchen."

As I said earlier, I now see that this time frenzy is shared by so many in our culture that mine is not simply a personal, family-induced addiction. But I would venture that each of us who is hooked is somehow hooked not only by the culture but by some personal hurts in our own lived experience that we need to root out if we are to be free.

One more story. My personality is such that I love seeing the big picture and putting new things together. Details bore me, and I sometimes find the doing of household tasks onerous to the point of pain. My mother-in-law is different. She loves housework, and sometimes even cleans house when something is bothering her, as a form of therapy. Once when she was visiting our home, she was doing some laundry, and I watched her peacefully folding towels. She was smiling, and moved with ease and grace, almost like Baryshnikov. When the towels were finished, they were so neat they could have been just taken out of the original package, and I could see Mom's satisfaction with a job well done.

The next time I did the laundry something amazing happened. I found myself immersed in the experience, enjoying the warmth and softness and sweet smell of the towels, enjoying the movement of my body as I smoothed them. I noticed that if I put the big towels on the bottom, the face towels in the middle of the pile, and the hand towels on top, that the pile was more stable and looked nicer than if I just piled them up in the order in which they happened to come out of the drier. And in the middle of this process, just when I noticed I was enjoying myself and became surprised and pleased by that, I heard a voice. It was not a true auditory hallucination, but the voice seemed real and not my own voice. It said, "I have come that you might have life, and have it more abundantly" (Jn. 10:10).

I realized then that if I were able to take all of the tasks that I find onerous, and do them with that sort of ease and grace and enjoyment in the doing for its own sake, that my life would be transformed. I am not at the point where I am doing this all the time, but I am sometimes gifted with minutes or hours of doing it, and I pray that as I age I will more and more live in the here-now.

This experience of being here now is what I think St. Paul referred to when he told his followers to pray without ceasing. For Paul recognized,

Revelations on the Road

whether consciously or not, that being fully with God happens only when we are fully in the moment. It is finding kairos in chronos. For God is found, this side of the Jordan, only in the moment where one actually resides.

One cannot force this to happen, but one can, like a farmer, cultivate the land so as to create the conditions in which the seed is most likely to grow. Here are some of the ways that I have found to cooperate in the process of being here now.

1. Breathing.

We have referred before to breath prayer, but have not explored it so far. It can be done in many ways, some of which I will describe briefly. The simplest is just to attend to one's breathing, with the awareness somewhere that breath is exchange with spirit (remember that breath and spirit are the same word in many languages of the world). I find this especially helpful when I am in a situation where my attention is also needed elsewhere: at a meeting, when reading, or working in ways that use my active, rational mind. The breath can be a constant, right brain prayer going on around and in the interstices between thoughts.

One can time the breathing with a formal prayer, such as the Jesus prayer. That particular prayer began somewhere back in the unwritten history of the early church, and can be traced to two stories in the eighteenth chapter of Luke's gospel. In the first, a tax collector pleaded for God's grace, calling, "God, be merciful to me, a sinner," in the second a blind man calls, "Jesus, Son of David, have mercy on me." What has evolved as the "long form" of the prayer is: "Jesus Christ, Son of the Living God, have mercy on me, a sinner." It can be shortened: "Jesus, have mercy" (*Christe Eleison* in Greek); or even just the name "Jesus."

Ron DelBene (1996) has developed a form especially for use with those who are very ill or dying. The pray-er chooses her favorite name for God, combines it with her deepest prayer, and plays with the words until they have a comfortable rhythm. Some examples: "Father/Mother fill me with your love;" "Jesus stay within my heart;" "Spirit keep me in your love;" "Jesus heal me with your power;" "Best Friend walk the way with me." Then pray your prayer with the rising and falling of your breath.

With these examples of breath prayer, you are free to develop your own. In this as in all things, be gentle with yourself and pray as you can, not as you can't.

2. <u>Slowing down; stopping between activities</u>

I often live at such a frenzied pace that my interior has no peace. But hurry is violence one commits on oneself. (Hurrying others has the same effect on them.) Simply slowing my steps slightly, slowing my movements, helps me to center, to be in the moment, and to enjoy the simple experience of living in my body and in space. It helps in learning to live abundantly.

My frenzy has often been apparent to others. Once a student gave me a poem, in an act which took some courage on her part, as she was not sure if I would receive it as a gift or an insult. Fortunately for both of us, I did the former. Let me share it with you:

Slow Me Down, Lord

Slow me down, Lord.
Ease the pounding of my heart by the quieting of my mind.
Steady my hurried pace with a vision of the eternal reach of time.
Give me, amid the confusion of the day, the calmness of the ever
    lasting hills.
Break the tensions of my nerves and muscles with the soothing
    music of the singing streams that live in my memory.
Help me to know the magical, restoring power of sleep.
Teach me the art of taking minute vacations—of slowing down to
    look at a flower, to chat with a friend, to pat a dog, to read a
few   lines from a good book.
Slow me down, Lord, and inspire me to send my roots deep into
    the soil of life's enduring values that I may grow toward the
    stars of my greater destiny.

(Note: My copy attributes this to Wilferd A. Peterson, but has no other citation.)

Revelations on the Road

3. Smile

Have you ever seen the picture of an Indian or oriental sage in meditation with a little half-smile upon his face? If not, think of the Mona Lisa. That little half smile is something you can cultivate. The muscles that create it seem somehow to be connected to the peaceful center we all have in us, even if we haven't spent much time there. I have discovered that not only does residing there cause the smile, the smile itself can be a vehicle for helping us to find that center. Play with it and see for yourself.

4. Mantram

Originating as a Hindu term that refers to a sacred word or formula embodying a form of the divine, the mantram has power to center one and bring the mind to stillness and peace, the word mantram (or mantra) has come to mean any prayer word that is repeated over and over.

Herbert Benson (1990) reports on research that shows that the repetition of any word, with slowed breathing and focused attentiveness to the word, has the power to bring altered states of consciousness as measured in altered brain activity. This has beneficial results apart from any explicitly religious or spiritual advantage—including such things as reductions in blood pressure and in the levels of chemicals connected with stress. But the subjective experience for one consciously on a spiritual pilgrimage is that of resting in the moment and being present with and to God.

5. Noticing/mindfulness/awareness

A concept, hard to grasp if one hasn't experienced it but important on the spiritual journey, is that of awareness or mindfulness. Anthony de Mello, an Indian Jesuit, called it awareness. Hindu and Buddhist teachers call it mindfulness. Some psychologists call it "noticing."

Whatever one calls it, it is a process whereby one becomes aware of the "I" as the observer self. You can get a sense of this by imagining that you are floating up out of your body and observing yourself. You might have a line of commentary going on: "Look at her. She is pretty upset right now. Isn't that a good 'cry'? Boy, she hasn't had one like that in a long time."

114

Or, as Thich Nhat Hahn (1976) suggests: wash the dishes to wash the dishes. Be present to the warmth of the sudsy water. Don't miss a detail of the richness of your life experience. Noticing, mindfulness, awareness is the opposite of grasping, trying, hurrying, shaping, controlling. It is simply the pure experience of what is. Being mindful all the time, if not what is meant by enlightenment, is at the very least an essential component of the experience of being enlightened.

I once mentored a group in which one of the members spoke of her effort to be more contemplative. She said "I am so rushed that even when I do stop to pray, I find that I am "doing my being." I thought a minute, and got an insight that is what Thich Nhat Hahn was talking about. I said, "Perhaps we are called rather to 'be our doing.'"

6. Using negative emotions as triggers to growth.

If we are practicing mindfulness, we are pretty free of expectations, not only of others, but of ourselves as well. It does not mean we do not have negative emotions. De Mello, in his tapes on awareness (1989) says, "Before I was enlightened, I used to get depressed. Since I am enlightened, I still get depressed." The difference is that he is able to observe the depression and allow it to trigger him to growth.

I am growing in my ability to recognize and utilize the element of choice in my reactions to things. I have found that, if I pay close attention, there is usually (perhaps always) a moment, sometimes just a tiny space, between an experience and my reaction to it, a moment in which I have a choice about my reaction.

I was once driving through a low income section of a town, and a young man of different ethnic background than mine came up and hit my car with his fist. I got angry. Later, upon reflection, I realized I had choice: I could have felt sadness at the conditions of his life that led him to anger; I could have seen the humor in the situation; I could have felt many things. My reflection gave me new awareness of choice. It led to prayer for him, for our society, for greater awareness of options for dealing with things that

Revelations on the Road

come to me so that I can best act for the health and wholeness of all concerned. In my journal I wrote:

Aware of anger against young man who hit my car. That would have been a good opportunity to practice mantram and love. (Better to recognize the missed opportunity than not to have done so. Better yet to recognize the opportunity at the time it happens. Best to act on it immediately. Oh, God, continue to teach me.)

Mindfulness is learned first in meditation, where one can practice it without distractions. Then it can become a way of life. Ram Dass says that almost anyone can become holy in an ashram. But can one keep equanimity in the midst of the city? I say begin where you are, and, gently, keep on moving.

MAKING THE STORY YOUR OWN

◆ List your current "have tos" in a column. Next to that column, make a second column for "if I don't, then what?" Could you live with the result of each? Might there even be some gift in it?

◆ In your life, what is the "one thing necessary"? What might you need to let go of (or take on) in order to obtain that one thing? Or might it be a free gift?

◆ When have you experienced the sense of wonder that happens when you are in the "oh" of nOw? Think back to the circumstances and revisit them, giving thanks for each.

◆ Try whichever of the methods of mindfulness are new to you. Consider using each for a week or more so you can really develop the habit of using it. Which of them works for you? Come up with your own list of mindfulness practices that can help you to learn to pray without ceasing.

FOR FURTHER READING

Bacovin, Helen. (Tr.) 1978. *Way of A Pilgrim*. Garden City, New York: Image Books.

Benson, Herbert. 1990. *The Relaxation Response*. New York: Avon.

Dass, Baba Ram. 1971. *Be Here Now*. New York: Crown Publishers.

Dass, Ram. 1990. *Journey of Awakening*. New York: Bantam Press.

DelBene, Ron et. al. 1996. *The Breath of Life: A Simple Way to Pray*. Nashville: The Upper Room.

Keyes, Ken. 1990. *The Handbook to Higher Consciousness*. Emeryville, CA: Publishers Group West.

Lawrence, Brother. 1977. *Practice of the Presence of God*. Garden City, New York: Image.

May, Gerald. 1991. *Addiction and Grace*. San Francisco: HarperSanFrancisco.

Schaef, Ann Wilson. 1990. *Meditations for Women Who Do Too Much*. San Francisco: HarperSanFrancisco.

Part 4:
You Cannot Go It Alone

Revelation Eleven: Community, Friendship, Marriage and the Body of Christ

Independence, Dependence and Interdependence

The primary values held by a people can be found in the names of their organizations and the titles of their documents. The major document connected to the founding of the United States of America is the Declaration of Independence. The very considerable value which we place on independence has been the source of innumerable gifts to us in this

Revelations on the Road

country, both collectively and individually. I personally am grateful beyond words for this gift. It allows me to think freely, speak freely, and act freely in a way unknown to the vast majority of humans over the course of history, and still not available in many parts of the world today.

But there is a shadow side to the value we place on independence. It prevents us from seeing and appreciating the gift of community. It allows us the illusion that we are independent, self-reliant and self-made. It devalues persons who see themselves and are seen by others as dependent. It is blind to the interdependence that is our true condition.

I was made aware of this one day when I was speaking in front of a large audience. That is an experience that can buttress your illusion of being independent and in control. There you are, choosing your own words and speaking them in your own way, with a rapt audience drinking them in. They sit quietly and listen. If you ask them to take a break, they stand up and do so. If you ask them to get into small groups, they do. You are clearly *in charge*.

I happened to glance at the plastic coffee cup I carry almost everywhere I go. All of a sudden, thousands if not millions of persons paraded through my mind. There was Juan Valdez, coffee grower in the Andes. There was the American (no doubt) advertising person who thought him up, and the many real South Americans whom he caricatured. There were workers in the coffee fields, makers of burlap bags, growers of the material for the bags, weavers, sewers, shippers. There were boat designers and builders and sales persons and operators. There were stevedores and truckers and accountants. There were those who invented the decaffination process, those who designed and built the factories to implement it, and all those involved in everything needed that allowed materials for building those plants to get there in a timely fashion. There were oil geologists and drillers and pipe-layers and plastics researchers and plastics injection-mold builders and operators, and an artist—who created the design on my cup. All these, and countless more, working so that I could have a cup of coffee in my hand and do my independent thing.

The talk happened to be on the spirituality of later life. One of the most dreaded things for older adults is the possibility of becoming dependent. So I spoke about this issue—the illusion of independence and dependence, and tho underlying true reality for all of us—interdependence. Even the solitary fur trappers in America's wide open west during the nineteenth century were dependent on those who bought the furs and those who brought the coffee and beans and sugar and flour and bacon they needed for their survival.

When I was a first year college student I moved from Erie, Pennsylvania, a town where I was known by most of the people I encountered during the course of an average day, to New York City. I found myself feeling an incredible lightness and freedom. I was no longer under observation by others who put controls on my behavior. I was utterly free to do exactly as I pleased. It felt as if all of the structures which had controlled me in the past had been lifted, and that only my own desires and values determined what I would or wouldn't do. I didn't want to do anything all that unconventional; but having the freedom to do almost anything was a heady, wonderful and almost palpable sensation. I believed firmly, as a child of the sixties, that I was and should be free to do anything I wished, as long as it didn't hurt others. And I was quite narrow in my definition of hurt.

Eight years later Kitty Genovese was brutally assaulted in the streets of Brooklyn, raped and killed during the course of a forty-five minute attack. She did not go gently into that good night; she fought back and screamed and made lots of noise. *But no one intervened!*

I could understand why no one would come rushing out of an apartment, shaking a finger at the killer and saying, "Now stop that, you naughty man." But I could not understand why thirty-six people, who were later interviewed and acknowledged hearing the attack, did not even pick up the phone to call the police. I spent a lot of time thinking about that.

What I finally realized is that in this world there is a terrible tension between freedom and social control. You either live in a world in which you have a supportive network that both sustains you and puts some controls on your behavior, or you have the freedom to live, and die, alone. This is not an absolute choice—no one is entirely alone. But the tension exists.

I believe that our nation has moved too far in the direction of independence. The price for all of us is intolerable. Families are trapped into thinking they have to do everything alone because they are independent, and they end up shredded by individual responsibilities that as a species we are probably made to share in community: feeding, clothing, educating, healing and entertaining ourselves and our children. People suffer terribly from the terror of somehow not measuring up and thereby becoming one of "those people who need help."

Those who have some condition that allows them and others to label them as dependent suffer from drastically reduced self-esteem. And the gifts they have to offer are often neither recognized nor received, forcing them into greater and greater isolation.

You can see this most starkly in institutions for those we label as dependent. The overwhelming characteristic of much institutional life is loneliness. This is true at least in what I have seen in prisons, many nursing homes, hospitals for the mentally ill and mentally retarded, and institutions for dependent and neglected or delinquent children. What is loneliness? It is the sense of being isolated from other people. But institutions are full of other people! The problem is that those in charge, and those whose policies have put them there, do not see residents (inmates, patients) as fully human. Hence residents do not see each other as fully human either, and therefore usually cannot be sources for assuaging the pains of loneliness for each other.

ANOTHER VISION

When I think of who I am, I realize that even what I think of as my very being is in a real sense almost entirely dependent on others. I could give you another litany of those responsible, but will mention just two groups that seem incidental, but are not: those who fought for the freedom for women to be educated and those who invented glasses. (As an almost addictive reader, who I am is largely shaped by what I have read; and without glasses I would be illiterate.)

But even if I exclude those whose personal influence is something of which I am not directly aware, I am left with an enormous debt. You already know about some of those I owe—my parents, my husband, and Clair to name but four. Let me tell you a little more about Clair as a way of illustrating some of the many levels of mystery that rest in relationship.

I have already told you that Clair led me to prayer, taught me about coincidence, and continues to exert a positive influence on my life, even though at this writing she has been dead for over eight years. The story I am going to share can be explained in many ways. I am not going to try to explain it, or explain it away, but to simply to share it as a way of asking a question into which you might enter. First the story.

Clair died on August 16th, 1994. Shortly afterwards I was on a team that put on a Cursillo weekend in the Episcopal Diocese of Arkansas. (Cursillo is a renewal movement in the Roman Catholic, Episcopal, and Lutheran denominations, known as Walk to Emmaus in the United Methodist church, and by other names in other groups.) It consists of a weekend retreat where participants hear talks by lay people and clergy on the essence of what it is to be a Christian. In small groups participants explore this for themselves. There are all kinds of surprises at Cursillo, lots of music, wonderful food, and immersion in an ocean of love and prayer from the many people who help put it together. One of the symbols used in Cursillo is the rainbow.

Clair was deeply involved in Cursillo and loved it as a concrete way of sharing her faith and giving gifts to others. So when I was on a team very shortly after her death, I told the rest of the team something about our relationship. Then I did something I had never done before and which surprised, and I think shocked, even me. Having never related to saints in anything other than a learning-from-them mode, I invoked Clair's prayers for the success of the Cursillo, asking that the Holy Spirit would be active among us,

Revelations on the Road

and that those who came would be touched in exactly the way God had in mind for them.

Our Cursillo was held on Petit Jean Mountain, a lovely site in central Arkansas with a view that helps one sense the wonder and beauty in creation. When we arrived for the first team meeting, we had come through a thunderstorm. The mountain was surrounded by the most amazing display of thick, black clouds with holes in them through which streams of sunlight streamed. Patches of blue sky decorated the dome of the sky like bows on a present. And just off the edge of the mountain was a double rainbow, more intense than any I had ever seen, with black clouds on both sides, and bright, white light between the two bows. We stood in silence and in awe for a long time, then walked inside to hold our meeting.

Sydney Murphy, the woman who was in charge of the planning, told us that this was her fifth Cursillo team. She had tried at each of the previous four to get a rainbow colored hot-air balloon to fly up from the valley below at the closing of the Cursillo as a surprise and gift for everyone involved. Somehow it had never worked out. This time, with all the details to handle, she couldn't even make the effort. But this rainbow was a gift to us to encourage us as we prepared.

At the closing of the Cursillo five rainbow colored hot air balloons came up the face of the mountain! It was a surprise and a gift that I will never forget. When I told a friend this story, I ended it by saying, "and this happened without *anyone* arranging it!" My friend smiled a mysterious smile, and asked, "What about Clair?" That is a question I will never even try to answer, but I love the question.

More recently I felt a nudge to get involved somehow in work with the poor. That used to be my paid work—first in foster care in New York City, then in Erie, Pennsylvania in a specially funded multi-problem-family project. But the work I had been doing in Arkansas had been largely in and through the church community, and the mainline churches there are mostly middle-class (and, unfortunately, mostly White). I lived in Pine Bluff, Arkansas, which,

126

though a town of only fifty-seven thousand and some souls, was the center of a complex of prisons—five to be exact. It seemed that perhaps prison ministry in some form might make sense.

Kairos (the same word that means a special moment in Greek) is a prison ministry that evolved from the Cursillo movement in this country. Certain prisoners, selected because they are leaders within the inmate community, are given the experience of a weekend in which they are inundated with a variety of messages of love. Afterwards they are encouraged to meet weekly with others who have shared the experience for prayer and mutual support (along with some "free world" volunteers from the Kairos ministry). The program has been enormously successful both in changing lives and in improving the quality of life in the prisons where it has been tried. One must have been through Cursillo (or a variant thereof) to be on a Kairos team, and that fit for me.

I reached out to those I knew were involved in Kairos, prayed about it, and felt a strong sense of rightness about being involved in this work. But nothing happened. A few months later I met two men who were involved in Kairos at a statewide event and told them of my interest. They said, "We've been talking about you in Kairos. We need women spiritual directors because there aren't enough women clergy involved. Would you have any interest in that?" I grinned and said, "That's sort of like asking an alcoholic if she wants a drink! The ministry that most moves my heart is spiritual direction, and I was the only lay spiritual director for Cursillo in the Diocese of Tennessee."

A week later I got a call from the lay leader of the next Kairos weekend. She said, "I hear you are interested in being on the team. Did you get my letter?" I had not. (It later surfaced in a pile of mail that had gotten lost after a vacation.) She told me the weekend dates, and my heart sank—I had agreed to be the keynote speaker at a conference in Tennessee on that very weekend.

The following day in an adult Sunday School class we spoke about how we felt God was nudging us to service. I told about my sense of call and my

disappointment and frustration in this Kairos business, and got an outrageous thought. I would call the organizer of the Tennessee conference and
ask if there was any possibility of changing the date.

Do you know the word *chutzpah?* It is Yiddish, and it means gall or
nerve. The classic example is the young man who killed both his parents in a
fit of rage and pleaded mercy from the court because he was an orphan!
Well, I have been accused of having more than my share of chutzpah, but
had never done anything that required more than that phone call.

When I called, the conference organizer told me that after we had
agreed on the date, he had contracted with the conference center and
three other speakers. I said that was fine; I would honor my commitment. I had
just needed to check it out to be faithful. The following morning he called me
back. He said that he had felt very ill at ease after our talk, sensing that I was
supposed to be on this Kairos team. He had checked with the conference
center and the other speakers, and all had agreed to change the date.

Writing in my journal the next day, I found myself writing a love letter to
Clair. In it I asked, "Did you have anything to do with the balloons and the
Kairos miracle?" She replied, "Yes and no. No because there's no manipula-
tion involved. Yes because we *are* all one—it's *us* doing it!"

I am not sure what she meant, but I know that I am more connected
on more levels with all of humanity, with all of creation, with the Creator,
than I can understand with my rational mind.

The church tries to talk about this using the term "the communion of
saints." In the *Book of Common Prayer* the term is described in the
Catechism (p.862):

> *Q. What is the communion of saints?*
> *A. The communion of saints is the whole family of God, the living*
> *and the dead, those whom we love and those whom we hurt,*
> *bound together in Christ by sacrament, prayer, and praise.*

It is easy to say these words, but hard to wrap the mind around them.
Let me tell you a story about something that helped me to do just that. One

day I was out running, and I began to pray for my friends. I began with a man in California, and in the middle of it, got sidetracked. I thought, "Strange. Galen is in California, right now, three hours ago! And Fran and Jay are in Colorado, right now, two hours ago. And Barbara is on an island in the Caribbean, right now, three hours from now. I do not have trouble believing that. So why should it be so hard to believe that others are still further away and in still weirder a time?" And I thought of those "gone before."

The letter to the Hebrews (Chapter 11) cites the heroism and faithfulness of a long list of saints, both Hebrew and Christian, and the deeds they did that demonstrated their faith. The author then goes on (12:1) to say, "Therefore, since we are surrounded by so great a cloud of witnesses, let us also . . . run with perseverance the race that is set before us."

Each of us can list our own personal cloud of witnesses. As I grow in age, I grow in the confidence that I am a drop in that cloud, and that the cloud is one, and that I cannot make it without that connection, and that, thank God, I do not have to.

KOINONIA (COMMUNITY)

The Greek word for community is *koinonia*. It is sometimes translated as fellowship. In the New Testament it implied a subjective sense of unity created by one-ness in the Spirit of God. It is something I have experienced, and appreciate more than words can say. Sometimes you meet someone and know that their life and yours are somehow tied together. It is not rational, but whenever I have had this sense, and have checked it out, the other person has felt it too, and attributes it to unity on a level below consciousness and beyond choice, based on our common love of God, and our common belief that God loves us. Jesus says, "By this everyone will know that you are my disciples, if you have love for one another" (Jn 13:35). It is true.

Likewise, and sadly, often people outside the church really do not believe our faith means anything, because we show so little love. I have been told that the reason Gandhi did not embrace Christianity is because he never met anyone who seemed to try to live it.

I have experienced this sense of *koinonia* in several contexts. One was during the 1960s at a New York City church that embraced the entire range of diversity present in that most diverse of cities. We had members who were African-American, Caucasian, Latino; we had people with no school experience at all, and others with multiple Ph.D.s. We had old and young, rich and poor. We had traditional Anglo-Catholics and people who had never attended church before, who came because we had a federally funded art program and because we acted welcoming. We had homeless people from the Bowery who slept in the church or church yard. And somehow it all worked. If we had any pride at all in who we were, it was pride in our diversity. It was exciting and fun and marvelous; if you looked around on a Sunday morning, it looked like the United Nations. It was what I believed the church was called to be.

After moving back to Erie when Frank and I were married, I learned that whether or not that was what the church was called to be, that's not what it was everywhere outside of the lower east side of New York! I went week after week because by that time the sacraments had become a necessity for me, but I didn't sense God's presence there. The experience was painful and disillusioning.

Then I met Helen Klauk, who in many ways is my spiritual mother. Helen and her husband, Herman, are living their lives as I think Jesus would have wanted them to do. They are generous, loving, and open. They have run the local soup kitchen one day a week for well over 30 years so that the Sisters of St. Benedict, who manage it the other six days, can have a day off once a week.

When I told Helen how difficult it was for me to sense God in the church, she smiled and said, "Because of the hypocrites?" I nodded, my eyes filling with tears, so glad to be understood. This loving woman shocked me, however, with her next comment. She shook her finger in my face and said, "Lynn, the church is not a hall of fame for saints. It is a hospital for sinners. And believe me, dear, you need it!"

Helen did not leave me there. She took me to the Hood Conference that summer. There I experienced that same sense of community, *koinonia*, as I had at St. Mark's, and it sustained me through the 51 weeks between "Hoods." There was an acceptance offered to each person who came; each was honored and held to be special and treated like a brother or sister.

Helen also introduced me to Cursillo and sponsored me for my own Cursillo weekend. I loved it, as I have already said. But this was not the major learning. Some months after I went to Cursillo, I was invited to be on my first team. It was there that I became aware of the power of communal prayer. For there is a large group of people, some scattered all over the world, who commit to pray for people who are going to Cursillo, and for those on the teams that put them on.

When I went through the weekend as a participant, I sensed wonderful things happening, but didn't attribute it to anything special. When I was on the team, I came to understand it as the power of the people of God united in prayer. I could literally feel myself floating on what felt like a river of prayer. One way to describe it is that there was an almost visceral sensation of being a part of the entire, worldwide Body of Christ.

These special experiences have given me a referent for what it means to be in *koinonia*. I wish it deeply for all persons, and especially for each of you.

BENEDICTINE SPIRITUALITY FOR NON-MONASTICS: MORE UNDERSTANDING OF COMMUNITY

For something over thirty-five years I have known and loved Benedictines. I have visited in at least eighteen monastic communities and have met members of dozens of others. I could write an entire book on what I have learned and how I have grown spiritually from Benedictines. Here I would speak only of their gifts to my understanding of community, which can be summed up in the three words of their vows: obedience, stability and *conversatio morum* (a phrase impossible of exact translation, which means the commitment to let one's life be constantly turned upside down by new understandings that come from God, other persons and events).

Obedience:

When I was baptized at the age of 22, several people recommended that I read Thomas a Kempis's *Imitation of Christ*; someone even gave me a copy. I trusted the donor, and tried to read it, but after several heroic attempts I had not made it past the first few chapters. (Since then I think I may have finished it, but it still has not become a favorite.)

My problem had to do with what I saw as Thomas's understanding of human nature. I am NOT a worm! I am a human being. God created me, created all of us, and said when that was done, "This is good; it is very good!"

I had worked for a long time to build up self-esteem and to love myself. Kempis seemed to say that this was a sinful attitude. I wrote him off, assuming others had somehow been misled by the clamor of voices praising him over the years.

I have not gone back to the book in many years, and may never do so. But I have come to a 180 degree turn on two words that he emphasizes, and which are also central to Benedictine spirituality: obedience and its inseparable sister, humility. At one time humility meant either humiliation (and I do think that it sometimes is a necessary prerequisite for humility), or a false modesty.

An image I now like for humility looks at it as the process of taking my camera, which usually is focused close up and personal on me, and zooming back so that the scene is viewed from God's perspective. There one sees everyone with the heart of the One who created them, who gave them gifts, who wants their highest good (which, not incidentally, results in the highest good of the whole Body as well), and who grieves their conflicts, differences and misunderstandings.

From that perspective one yearns to do the thing that will bring about God's will, and is able to voluntarily sacrifice short term self-interest in the cause of the good of all. One can see how the gifts given are meant to be used; one can have compassion on those who have missed this view; one can love with God's love. This perspective gives spaciousness and freedom in one's choices. It is not humiliation, but rather strength and joy and love and power (albeit power of a different sort than the power that is celebrated in the media).

Obedience relates to humility, in fact is the action that results from that perspective. The word *obedience* comes from the same root as the word *listen*. I had known that before, but had heard it somehow as "Listen to me, young lady, and do as I tell you!" The behavior which follows that kind of listening somehow feels like self-abuse. But the obedience that results from a change in perspective, a transformation of desire, feels more like profound self-fulfillment.

In the Rule of Benedict there is a lot of discussion of obedience. First and foremost is obedience to God. "Prefer nothing whatever to Christ," Benedict advises near the end of the Rule. Second is obedience to the Abbess or Abbot who is to be obeyed as if she or he were Christ himself. But it does not end there. Benedict advises elsewhere in the Rule that the monastic is to be obedient to all the other monastics, even to the very old and to the very young, even to the sick and to the guest. In words similar to those found in the Episcopal Baptismal covenant (*Book of Common Prayer*), the monastic is to "seek and serve Christ in all persons." And this requires that one listen to them all.

One can even listen for Christ in non-human things: pets and waterfalls and junk heaps. My dog's eager attentiveness, tail-wagging, eyes on me, waiting only for my word to "sit," "lie down," "come" or "stay" used to be a model for how I would like to be with God. Listening to that wonderful dog brought me to greater obedience.

The waterfall says (speaking for God), "look how beautiful I am! I keep on coming, full of water. Drink what you need, but don't try to grasp or you

Revelations on the Road

will drown. There is more where this is coming from, and you can trust that I will be here for you." Listening to the waterfall can free me from fearfully clutching things to my bosom.

A young woman with whom I did spiritual direction once spoke of walking through an area at an Arkansas retreat house where there was remnant devastation from the tornado of a couple of years earlier. Among the downed trees was a strange mix of new growth and human debris. In a rusted Maxwell House coffee can was a mix of soil and baby plants—an Easter rooted in the Good Friday of the storm. Listening to the coffee can, she was able to open some of the debris in her own life to God's healing attention.

Seeking and serving Christ perhaps not just in all other persons, but in all things, might be the ultimate in obedience. Pray for that for yourself and for all of us.

Stability:

In our nation, where the average person moves every five years and the average marriage is as likely to end in divorce as to fulfill the promise "until death do us part," the vow of stability seems either quaint or very appealing, depending on how sick we are of the fickleness and ever accelerating rate of change in our lives. Perhaps "new" is not an unmitigated blessing!

The community, for a Benedictine nun or monk, is the locus for the living out of vows. One Benedictine elder I interviewed described it as "the place both of our wounding and of our healing." On our sabbatical I was struck over and over how the fulfilled promise to sit, three to seven times a day, facing half—and shoulder to shoulder with the other half—of one's lifetime community, whether one is at peace with them, at loggerheads, or indifferent, and praying together as in one voice, embodies the commitment to stability. Eating meals together, in silence or in conversation, does likewise. (It also embodies both the cost and the gift of stability.)

How many people have you known who leave their church at the time of divorce, just at the time when to stay might allow both members of the former couple to find a way to live in community (if not in marriage), together in the sight of God and their Christian brothers and sisters? They thus do not find the gift: the way for healing to follow wounding.

How many people have you known who avoid any social occasion at which they are likely to be confronted with someone who has wounded them, or whom they have wounded? One friend of mine once quit a dearly beloved social club for the sole reason that an antagonist attended it, too. What a difference there might be if we made a commitment of stability to the organizations that support things we love! How might we learn that in that commitment we can find reconciliation and healing? Instead we flee from confrontation and reinforce the destructive pattern of leaving before we find the gift. (Ken Keyes divides people into two groups: our lovers and our teachers. How many lessons we miss by insisting on adding "enemies", a category that allows us to dismiss their teaching.)

I once had a quadriplegic student who was contemplating marriage. He feared that it might end in divorce, and asked me what I thought made a marriage likely to succeed (or at least last). I thought a while, and came up with two major things: 1) that the needs the two meet in each other are long term needs, rather than terribly intense but short-term needs, and 2) that they make a commitment. Having done so, when (not if) they run into trouble and hard times, the question becomes "How are we going to work this out?" rather than whether we are. That is what the monastic has basically committed to: working it out.

This changes our perspective, so that problems and troubles, rather than being an interruption, are a way of overcoming ego, of experiencing the discipline of perseverance, and finally of becoming holy.

In our society, so many of us flee at the first sign of wounding. Thus we lose the gift of healing inherent in a community of commitment. This applies to our marriages, our workplaces, our churches, and many of our other commitments. We can learn much from the Benedictines about how to live community life, if we will.

Conversatio Morum:

Conversatio Morum is the third of the Benedictine vows. The translation which seems to capture it best for me is "ongoing conversion of life." There are two aspects of this on which I want to focus. First is the idea that conversion is not a one time event in life but the very nature of life in Christ itself. Second is the understanding that the daily events of life offer us all we need in the way of tools, *if* we are only willing to receive them for that purpose, and are able to pay attention.

As a young person I thought conversion was like a wedding: you got the idea, you came together with others in a public ceremony, and then you were "finished." You lived happily ever after.

I have learned that conversion is, rather, like marriage. You need the impetus of the formal ceremonial promise, the support of the community, and the sacramental blessing, in order to have the strength and tools to create the marriage, a life-long task. The same is true with life in Christ.

Another way to think of conversion is as a two-step process, the first is short—a recognition of one's unavoidable need for God. The second is long—an ongoing realization that God has a need for *me*, and that I must be willing to undergo the lifelong process of being reformed into the image of God's Beloved so that I can do what is needed.

The two are not as separate as this makes it sound. Daily, in the humiliations of discovering how far short we fall of the ideal to which we aspire, we learn we need God's grace and healing and forgiveness in order to survive at all. So we turn (con-vert) yet again to ask for it.

But as we discover those gifts, more and more we yearn to share them with others, so that all may be blessed. It is in that yearning that we discover God's need for us—to be the hands and hearts and eyes and ears and feet and hands of Christ's body to the world.

I served as a volunteer chaplain for several years at the jail in Pine Bluff. That was a microcosmic experience of this whole journey for me. I went because I believed from prayer and pondering that somehow God wanted me there. I went knowing how inadequate I felt—a married, middle class, not-having-suffered-much, White, Episcopal woman from the north trying to speak God's word of love to mostly non-married, non-middle class, having-suffered-much, Black-White-Hispanic, definitely non-Episcopal, mothers from the south. What could I say to connect with their life experience? How could I avoid playing the fool or coming across as holier than thou? How could I teach and pray in a way that met their need?

The secret in Pine Bluff is the same as it is everywhere—namely, in taking my eyes off me. Rather I must ask how God can work to connect with the life experience of those with whom I am called to work (parenthetically, through me).

Yet when I got there, amazingly almost every time, God did a miracle. Some-unknown-blessed-how, the women in that "God-forsaken" place saw God's love in me. And I saw God's love in them! Thinking I had gone to offer, I discovered that I had gone to receive. God prayed through them, connecting with my life experience. God taught through them, in a strange way that simultaneously humbled me and blessed me. And so I discovered my need, and discovered that I am to be God's instrument in the same moment. I sought and served Christ in them; I was sought and served by Christ in them.

Throughout the Christian journey this happens over and over and over. I drive onto the highway, concerned to get where I am going. And someone pulls over to avoid the almost-accident that I didn't even see coming. I discover again that I have put myself in the center of the universe, and repent. I realize I have been saved and give thanks.

I get impatient with my husband, and then learn of some of the pressures of his day. I discover again that I have put myself in the center of the universe, and repent.

I sit in my prayer place in the morning, reflecting in mind and journal on the day before, and discover the myriad of ways in which God has gifted me during the previous twenty four hours, and give thanks. I discover the invitations not noticed, and repent. I notice the way nature has surrounded the various moments of the day with the glories of God—in birds, sunset, moon-rise, snow or rain, and give praise.

Conversatio morum. Hard to translate. But providing a gift of awareness of the process of ongoing transformation that never ends until (perhaps) we cross the Jordan. Let the idea help you to receive the daily gifts, respond to the daily opportunities for thanksgiving, praise, repentance, and perhaps above all renewal of your awareness of how utterly dependent you are and how utterly reliable is God's steadfast love. And give thanks.

FRIENDSHIP

I believe that friendship may be the most unappreciated gift we have. It is a miracle that it ever happens, for so many factors conspire to prevent it—especially in our post-modern, mobile, highly insular culture. Thank God for adolescence, the time when we are so wired that the peer group assumes monumental proportions in the landscape of our reality. For during adolescence we come to learn something about being best friends. We taste the sweet wine of listening and being listened to, of having our words cherished and our company enjoyed for nothing but its own sweet sake. We relish caring about the minutia of what feel like the daily crises of our friends and having that caring returned.

For once we leave the protection of our school environment, we are pried away from friends by the pressures of work and homemaking and community service. Too-close friendships are looked at askance. If they are across gender lines, they are viewed with suspicion as a threat to marriage (for those married) or a stage on the way to marriage (for the single). If they are same-gender friendships, sometimes others wonder about our sexual orientation.

The culture conspires to keep us skidding on the surface of relationships with non-family members like waterbugs on a pond: "How are you . . . ;" "Fine, fine. Busy, busy. . . ;" "Yes, isn't it something? We must get together sometime . . . ;" "I just can't believe how long it's been."

138

So when a Clair comes along, it behooves us to pay attention, to nourish the relationship, to pray for God to bless it, and to do what needs to be done to make it possible for it to survive.

In *The Sacred Dimensions of Women's Experience* (Gray, 1988), there is a chapter by Linda Weltner, entitled "There's No Kin Like Kindred Spirits," in which Weltner details the development of a most unusual friendship. Originating in a common desire to oppose the development of nuclear power in their community, and aware of the difficulty of managing the rest of the obligations in their respective lives, two women chose to help each other out with child care, shopping, and other details of life. This led eventually to a virtual merger of their two families, revolving around their friendship, but including their spouses and children. The riches of this friendship are wonderful to behold.

> *Lynn and I consider our friendship a sacrament, a celebration of all that gives our lives meaning and direction. We find in our friendship a reason for joy, a source of self-revelation, and a place of comfort (p. 16).*

I have written a poem celebrating friendship, that could fit this one which I know only through the printed page. In addition to Clair, for whom I wrote it, I have been blessed with others who are real friends, and have offered me the incredible treasure of their friendship.

FOR MY FRIEND

Friendship is a model of the love of God.
Being always free.
It has no bonds of marriage
No ties of physical union
No models, no social or legal supports.

It rests like a fragile and beautiful flower
On the continuing love and trust

Vibrating like a force field
Between the two
Who daily say their "yes" and
Call each other "friend."

That yes, with you, my friend
Brings me constant joy.
I offer daily thanksgiving for you
And for our love.

May the peace of God
Which passes all understanding
Be with each of us, and our friendship
Evermore. Amen.

CONJUGAL SPIRITUALITY

My marriage is the single most powerful, healing, scary, educational, exciting event in my life in this world. Frank has been influential in so many ways of which I am conscious, and perhaps more which are like an undercurrent in a river, carrying aspects of my life like boats unconscious of the water underneath. Although he was an atheist at the time, early in our relationship he so convinced me of my lovableness that I was able to love myself and begin to believe that indeed God might love me too.

We are very different. He is an off-the-scale introvert who has explicitly admitted that he is the most interesting person he knows. He wonders sometimes why people are so busy trying to meet hordes of others, when they can spend their time so well (or at least he can) in their own company. I am an off-the-scale extrovert. Between us that is more of a problem for him sometimes than for me: an introvert makes a wonderful audience for an extrovert!

Frank is one who makes decisions with his head; I with my heart. While it is easy for us to devalue one another (he is cold; I am fuzzy-minded), we have learned the gifts that can be added to the head-man in appropriating the wisdom of the heart, and to the heart-woman by enfleshing her compassion with logical and practical strategies for making loving things happen.

There are more differences. Our friends Andy and Carol Sloan have some of the same differences, and Carol has expressed it well in the story of their respective styles of shopping. Carol saves coupons, checks ads, reads Consumer Reports, drives to different stores to comparison-shop. She saves money and gets precisely what she wants. Andy walks into a clothing store, glances at the shirt rack, and says to the clerk (pointing at a simple Oxford shirt), "I'll take one of those in each color in my size."

Being so different, others were a little concerned about Frank and me when we told them we were thinking about getting married. (Thank God for lust; without it no one would ever take the risk of hooking up with someone different—and while not all couples are as different as we are, all *are* different.) Looking back after thirty-five years of marriage, a marriage which has gotten progressively better (with a few back-waters of confusion, pain and anger), I think a big part of the gift was the difference.

Frank and I have stretched and taught each other so much. And in all those years, while I have been at various times not only loving, happy and delighted but also frustrated, angry and hurt, there has not been one time when I have been bored! Once I wrote Frank a love poem. The verse I have in mind was written in thanksgiving for the wonder of sex. But since then the idea has generalized to any mutual sharing of love for and delight in each other (and, by extension, to any mutual sharing of love for and delight in *any* one). In sex, the move one makes out of one's own yearning and desire delights the other, whose response delights in turn. I wrote:

Giver's gift, received,
becomes a gift itself.

I have pondered for some time the nature of marriage. It is unique among all the relationships one has. It is hard to define. The Bible speaks of "two becoming one flesh" (e.g. Gn 2:24; Mt 19:5; Eph 5:31). I do not believe

Revelations on the Road

this is simply a metaphor for physical joining, although it includes that. Yet the two identities are not lost (or, if they are, something has gone awry).

A couple can fail to become one flesh in at least two ways: first by idolizing the other (i.e. putting the other in the place that should be reserved only for God), and second by refusing the vulnerability to the other that is required to become one flesh. Many couples seem to be anything but one flesh, simply living in the same house and acting a role, going through motions, essentially living alone. On the one hand, we can be so terrified of being alone that we submerge our own identity in that of the other. On the other hand, we can be so terrified of the loss of individual identity implied in a mistaken understanding of one flesh, that we avoid entering the mystery at all. For one flesh is not the dissolution of the two, but each allowing the emergence of a third entity in which each participates: for the sake of the other, and of the self, and for the service of the community (including children, if they should come).

THE TRINITY AS A MODEL FOR *KOINONIA*

Mary Anne McPherson Oliver (1994), to whom I owe the term *conjugal spirituality,* compares the conjugal relationship to the relationship among the three parts of the Trinity. I must confess that while the concept of Trinity served me well over the years as an intellectual construct upon which to hang my theology, until reading Oliver I had never felt a relationship to it. I related sometimes to the Father (or, in recent years and with more power, the Mother). I related sometimes to Jesus. I related to, or perhaps more accurately, was often aware of being *in* the Spirit. But the relationship among these three was something that I had not really thought about very much.

Shortly after reading Oliver, one day while praying I put the words of the Doxology to the tune of "Amazing Grace." Unless I distorted the melody, the second and fourth lines did not scan. So I modified the words. Here is how it came out:

Praise God from whom all blessings flow.
Praise God all creatures here.
Praise God above ye heavenly host.
Praise Trinity so dear.

All of a sudden I *felt* love for the Trinity! I was astounded. It is not possible to feel love for an intellectual construct. And this love I felt did not change the fact that the Trinity is still a mystery beyond my ability to understand. It is hard to put into words. But the notion of Trinity had taken on a relational quality.

Our close friends the Sloans include Carol and Andy (the parents), four children, five grandchildren, and three children in-law. We love them all. We love them individually. But we also love "the Sloans"—the mysterious entity made up of all these folks and more than the sum of them. Somehow "God the Father, God the Son and God the Holy Spirit" had become "The Trinity," an object of even more love than "The Sloans."

The Trinity, being relational within itself, somehow casts new light on the nature not only of marriage, but of friendship, of membership in all the entities of which we are a part, and of the Body of Christ. St. Paul speaks of the church as the Body of Christ, using very literal physical images to describe it and talking about our utter interdependence.

For just as the body is one and has many members; and all the
members of the body are one body, though many, so it is with
Christ. For in the one Spirit we were all baptized into one body—
Jews or Greeks, slaves or free—and we were all made to drink of
one Spirit. Indeed the body does not consist of one member, but
of many. If the foot would say, "Because I am not a hand, I do not
belong to the body," that would not make it any less a part of the
body. And if the ear would say, "Because I am not an eye, I do not
belong to the body," that would not make it any less a part of the
body. If the whole body were an eye, where would the hearing
be? If the whole body were an ear, where would the sense of smell

*be? As it is God arranged the members in the body, each one of
them, as God chose. If all were a single member, where would the
body be? As it is, there are many members, yet one body. The eye
cannot say to the hand, "I have no need of you," nor again the
head to the feet, " I have no need of you." On the contrary, the
members of the body that seem to be weaker are indispensable,
and those members of the body that we think less honorable we
clothe with greater honor, and our less respectable members are
treated with greater respect; whereas our more respectable members do not need this. But God has arranged the body, giving the
greater honor to the inferior member, that there may be no dissen-
sion within the body, but the members may have the same care
for one another. If one member suffers, all suffer together with it; if
one member is honored, all rejoice together with it. Now you are
the body of Christ, and individually members of it. (I Cor 12:12-27).*

This is powerful, counter cultural stuff. This is not raw individualism, naked
independence. This is being what one is, but being at one and the same
time incapable even of existence itself without the rest of the community. It
describes the nature of our Trinitarian God, and the nature of humankind
created in the very image of that God. It is reflected in our marriages, in our
families, in our friendships, in our churches, in our workplaces and in all our
communities of so many kinds and shapes and sizes. It is reflected in every
aspect of our entire existence. It is there whether we view ourselves as independent, dependent or interdependent.

My prayer is that we live the paradox, that we can both receive the
gifts that have come with the American understanding of independence,
and at the same time renew and rejoice in the ancient heritage of unity in
the body. I pray that the understandings of scientific ecology (enriched by
the sense of oneness with nature that we can learn from all native peoples)
may bring us back to our rightful place in the scheme of things. May new
humility prove a gift as well as a painful lesson, and lead us, individually and

corporately, to appreciation of the wonder of our unity. The Hebrew prayer I learned as a child shimmers with deepened meaning for me: "Shamah Yisroel, Adonoi Elohenu, Adonoi Echod; Hear Oh Israel, the Lord our God, the Lord is One." Amen,

MAKING THE STORY YOUR OWN

◆ What are your earliest memories of being independent? What were you told about the importance of being independent, and how did that translate into day-to-day life? How do you see the virtues of independence now?

◆ Who was the first person you knew who was dependent? What did this mean to you? In what ways have you been and are you dependent?

◆ Who are the Clairs in your life? How have you found ways to celebrate and nurture these friendships?

◆ What experiences have you had of being in community that were redemptive for you? What happened that made you aware of being a part of something larger than yourself? What difference does that make for your understanding of what life is about?

◆ If you are married, how would you describe the nature of that relationship? Has it ever been idolatrous? Has it been so scary that you took flight (emotionally or physically)? How might you celebrate your "one fleshedness"?

FOR FURTHER READING

Farnham, Suzanne G. et al. 1991. *Listening Hearts: Discerning Call in Community.* Harrisburg, PA: Morehouse.

Oliver, Mary Anne McPherson. 1994. *Conjugal Spirituality: The Primacy of Mutual Love in Christian Tradition.* Kansas City, MO: Sheed and Ward.

Vest, Norveen. 1990. *Preferring Christ: A Devotional Commentary and Workbook on the Rule of Saint Benedict.* Trabuco Canyon, CA: Source Books.

Epilogue
The Kin-dom of Heaven Is at Hand!

I had been waiting to finish this book, as I felt there ought to be an epilogue, but wasn't sure what it was supposed to say. As I write this it has been two days since what may prove in retrospect to have been the most important spiritual experience of my life. Before this past weekend, there were two passages of scripture that I had read with a certain amount of skepticism: 1) *It is no longer I who live, but Christ who lives in me* (Gal 2:20); and 2)

> *God is love, and those who abide in love abide in God, and God abides in them. Love has been perfected among us in this: that we*

may have boldness on the day of judgment, because as God is, so are we in this world. There is no fear in love, but perfect love casts out fear; for fear has to do with punishment, and whoever fears has not reached perfection in love. We love because God first loved us. Those who say, "I love God" and hate their brothers or sisters are liars, for those who do not love a brother or sister whom they have seen, cannot love God whom they have not seen. The commandment we have from God is this: those who love God must love their brothers and sisters (1 Jn 4:16b-21).

What made these come alive as a true description of a felt reality was a weekend spent as part of the Kairos team I described in the last chapter. I met many women in the prison, some of whose stories I learned a bit about. None of them would have been accepted in the "nice" circles in which I spend a lot of time. Most had had some experience with drugs, some selling. The least acceptable probably locked her children in a room and set fire to the house, at least that was what she had been convicted of doing. She was even rejected by her fellow inmates.

My reaction? It was most astonishing, for I felt absolutely no judgment whatsoever. All I felt was a flood of compassion. It was not sickly-sweet sympathy, but genuine compassion. I could see the pain, the lostness, the isolation, the self-condemnation, the hopelessness, the broken heart. And I loved with a love the likes of which I had never before experienced.

The women's and men's weekends were held simultaneously but in separate places. The women's finished first, and its team was invited to attend the closing for the men's retreat. The same thing happened to me there. One of the men, the biggest man I have ever seen in person, and so rough-looking that you'd cross the street to avoid him, told of having stalked and killed a family member in a pre-meditated act of revenge. Once in prison, he proceeded to build a thick emotional wall around himself, so as never to allow himself to be hurt any more. He had been deeply touched by the weekend, and planned to change his life, to become a force for

Epilogue

support and love among his fellow prisoners. Whatever he does in the future, I am convinced he was utterly sincere at that moment. And I would not be surprised to learn of miracles he accomplishes there in the future.

My eyes, in looking at these very rough, very "bad" men, felt as if they were on fire. I could literally feel love pouring through them. I could feel it pouring out of my heart as well. John Wesley is reported to have experienced a sensation he described as his heart being strangely warmed. My heart too felt on fire.

I have used a descriptive term to apply to Mother Teresa: a wind tunnel. If Spirit is indeed wind, breath and air, then when you are, in your own interior, free of your own "stuff," free enough to love the unlovable, you are a wind tunnel. God's love pours into you; you do not grasp it, but let it pour out to others. Whoosh!

I had said before "Mother Teresa is a wind tunnel, and I'm only a little fart!" Well, during my Kairos weekend experience, simply because I was willing to be made an instrument of God's love, *I became a wind tunnel!* I do not expect that I will never judge again. In fact, I was not entirely non-judgmental of my fellow team members. But where it was needed, and (I am convinced) because of my prayers—and the prayers of at least 100 others who had been asked to pray for me and for Kairos—where God needed me to be a wind tunnel, I was a wind tunnel! It was the most wonderful feeling in the world. Being loved unconditionally is the second most wonderful feeling in the world, and I have experienced it too at special moments (kairoses): from spiritual directors, from my husband, from Clair, from an occasional other. But this was the first time that there was no obstacle, not even a tiny one, to my own loving.

So now I know the truth of the words of Paul and John. We are to love one another as God loves us. Perfect love does cast out fear. Whether I could offer it if one of those inmates turned up on my doorstep is not the point. Where it exists, it casts out fear.

Now the witness of others comes to mind to support me: Dietrich Bonhoeffer, who faced death by hanging with a sense of peace because he had learned to love like that. Gandhi, who died with the name of God on his lips as he fell at the hands of an assassin. Martin Luther King Jr., who knew he was going to die, and did so willingly to show forth his unconquerable love of all, even his enemies. Many of the brothers and sisters in the early church, who died on crosses, in fire, torn apart by wild animals, or in other unimaginably horrible ways. And most of all, our brother Jesus, who said as he was being crucified "Forgive them, Father, for they know not what they do."

I leave this experience knowing I am not finished being transformed, but with the prayer that God will continue to transform me, to teach me to love without regard for the cost, as I stand trembling on the doorstep of the House of God.

You come too!

Notes

Revelation One

[1] I have modified quotations throughout this book to eliminate gender bias. In the case of this example, I am sure that Heschel would approve were he writing now. I have done this with all quotations, including those from scripture. I hope this is not distracting to you, but after a couple of decades of constant distraction at the masculine bias in so much of religious language, I decided not to participate in it in this book. For example, I render most of the masculine pronouns for God as "God." The significance of the incarnation is not that Jesus was male, but that he was human. If you find this disturbing, try what I do when the distraction pulls the other way: use it as an opportunity for mindfulness, or for charity toward the writer, or simply change the language in your own mind.

[2] All Biblical quotations, unless otherwise indicated, are from the New Revised Standard Version.

Revelation Four

[1] This was an invitational retreat put on at the St. Scholastica Center in Fort Smith, Arkansas by Sr. Macrina Wiederkehr and Sr. Joyce Rupp. They are interested in having their design replicated. For further information, contact Sr. Macrina at P.O. Box 3489; Fort Smith, AR 72913.

Revelation Five

[1] Frankl said this when he spoke at the Annual Program Meeting of the American Society on Aging held in Washington, D.C. in March of 1989.

Revelation Eight

[1] The words *meditation* and *contemplation* are sometimes used as synonyms. Their meanings in eastern and western religions are often reversed. We will use the western sense, where meditation is thoughtful reflection on a

topic related to God and our relationship to God. (The origin of the word is in a description of the process of a cow chewing its cud.) Contemplation, from a root meaning "to look at," is a wordless state of awareness of God's presence. It resembles adoration, as defined in this chapter.

[2] A mandala is a symbolic art work done in the shape of a circle, usually totally symmetrical. A rose window is an example of a mandala. Its purpose is to focus attention on the sacred.

Revelation Ten

[1] Education for Ministry is a program of continuing theological education for lay people (or clergy) designed by the School of Theology at the University of the South. It includes individual study and small group processing, designed to help all baptized Christians learn to effectively live out their faith in daily life. For more information contact Education for Ministry; University of the South; Sewanee, TN 37375.

[2] I write this with some concern about hurting my mother, who was totally without malice in this incident. There is no parent who raises a child without similar incidents, and probably most of them remain innocuous for the child. But in this case it did not.

REFERENCES

(Note: Where the reference has been republished since I read it, I am citing the most accessible source rather than the original edition.)

Anderson, Sherry R. and Patricia Hopkins. 1991. *The Feminine Face of God: The Unfolding of the Sacred in Women.* New York: Bantam.

Anonymous. 1978. *Way of A Pilgrim.* Translated by Helen Bacovin. Garden City, NY: Image Books.

Benson, Herbert. 1990. *The Relaxation Response.* New York: Avon.

Berman, Philip and Connie Goldman, Editors. 1992. *The Ageless Spirit.* New York: Ballantine.

Bloom, Anthony. 1988. *Beginning to Pray.* New York: Paulist Press.

Bohlen, Jean Shinolda. 1994. *Crossing to Avalon: A Woman's Midlife Pilgrimage.* San Francisco: HarperSanFrancisco.

Bonhoeffer, Dietrich. 1995. *The Cost of Discipleship.* New York: Simon and Schuster.

_____. 1972. *Letters and Papers from Prison.* New York: Macmillan.

Boulad, Henri. 1991. *All is Grace: God and the Mystery of Time.* New York: Crossroad.

Bray, Louise Hardin. 1988. "Body-Decisions as Sacred" in *Sacred Dimensions of Women's Experience.* Edited by Elizabeth Dodson Gray. Wellesley, MA: Roundtable Press.

Brooke, Avery. 1986. *Hidden in Plain Sight: The Practice of Christian Meditation*. Nashville, TN: The Upper Room.

Brown, Christy. 1991. *My Left Foot*. Portsmouth, NH: Heinemann.

Brownmiller, Susan. 1993. *Against Our Will: Men, Women and Rape*. Greenwich, CT: Fawcett.

Broyles, Anne. 1988. *Journaling: A Spirit Journey*. Nashville: The Upper Room.

Buechner, Frederick. 1985. *The Alphabet of Grace*. New York: Walker.

Campbell, Will. 1997. *Brother to a Dragonfly*. New York: Continuum.

Capon, Robert Ferrar. 1995. *The Third Peacock*. Published in *The Romance of the Word: One Man's Love Affair With Theology: Three Books*. San Diego, CA: Wm. B. Eerdmans Publishing Co.

Church Hymnal Corporation. 1979. *The Book of Common Prayer and Administration of the Sacraments and Other Rites and Ceremonies of the Church; Together with the Psalter or Psalms of David, According to the Use of The Episcopal Church*. New York: Church Hymnal Corporation.

Church Pension Fund. 1940. *The Hymnal of the Protestant Episcopal Church in the United States of America*. New York: Church Pension Fund.

Dass, Baba Ram. 1971. *Be Here Now*. New York: Crown Publishers.

Dass, Ram. 1990. *Journey of Awakening*. New York: Bantam Press.

De Caussade, Jean-Pierre. 1995. *The Fire of Divine Love : Readings from Jean-Pierre De Caussade*. Translated by Robert Llewelyn. Chicago: Triumph.

References

de Mello, Anthony, SJ. 1989. *Wake Up To Life.* Tapes produced by We and God Spirituality Center; Jesuit Hall at St. Louis University; 3601 Lindell Blvd; St. Louis, MO.

DelBene, Ron et al. 1996. *The Breath of Life: A Simple Way to Pray.* Nashville: The Upper Room.

DelBene, Ron et al. 1988. *Into the Light: A Simple Way to Pray with the Sick and the Dying.* Nashville: The Upper Room.

Edwards, Tilden. 1978. *Living Simply Through the Day.* New York: Paulist Press.

Evely, Louis. 1963. *That Man is You.* New York: Paulist Press.

Farnham, Suzanne G. et al. 1991. *Listening Hearts: Discerning Call in Community.* Harrisburg, PA: Morehouse.

Finley, James. 1980. *Merton's Palace of Nowhere.* Notre Dame, IN: Ave Maria Press.

Fischer, Kathleen. 1985. *Winter Grace.* New York: Paulist Press.

Foster, Richard. 1992. *Prayer: Finding the Heart's True Home.* San Francisco: HarperSanFrancisco.

Fowler, James. 1995. *Stages of Faith; The Psychology Of Human Development and the Quest for Meaning.* San Francisco: HarperSanFrancisco.

Frankl, Viktor. 1997. *Man's Search for Meaning, Revised and Updated Edition.* New York: Washington Square Press.

Revelations on the Road

Fulgum, Robert. 1993. *All I Really Need to Know I Learned in Kindergarten.* New York: Ivy Books.

Gilligan, Carol. 1993. *In A Different Voice: Psychological Theory and Women's Development.* Cambridge: Harvard University Press.

Goffman, Irving. 1962. *Asylums: essays on the social situation of mental patients and other inmates.* Chicago: Aldine Publishing Co. (Out of print but easily available in any university library.)

Gray, Elizabeth Dodson. Ed. 1988. *Sacred Dimensions of Women's Experience.* Wellesley, MA: Roundtable Press.

Green, Thomas, SJ. 1977. *Opening to God.* Notre Dame, IN: Ave Maria Press.

_____. 1984. *Weeds Among the Wheat.* Notre Dame, IN: Ave Maria Press.

_____. 1995. *When the Well Runs Dry.* Notre Dame, IN: Ave Maria Press.

Guenther, Margaret. 1995. *Toward Holy Ground: Spiritual Directions for the Second Half of Life.* Cambridge, MA: Cowley Press.

Hahn, Thich Nhat. 1976. *The Miracle of Mindfulness: A Manual of Meditation.* New York: Beacon Press. (Note: This is out of print but available on audio tape from Harper Audio.)

Harris, Maria. 1995. *Jubilee Time: Celebrating Women, Spirit, and the Advent of Age.* New York: Bantam.

Heschel, Abraham Joseph. 1997. *God in Search of Man: A Philosophy of Judaism.* New York: Noonday Press.

References

Hillesum, Etty. 1996. *Etty Hillesum : An Interrupted Life the Diaries, 1941-1943 and Letters from Westerbork.* New York: Henry Holt.

Hopkins, Gerard Manley. 1983. *Poems and Prose of Gerard Manley Hopkins.* Reprint Edition. New York: Viking Press.

Huber, Lynn W. 1985. *Connections: The Place of the Church in the Personal Networks of the Elderly.* Unpublished doctoral dissertqtion from the Case Western Reserve University. Available through University Microfilms International. Ann Arbor, MI.

Hurnard, Hannah. 1986. *Hinds Feet on High Places.* Wheaton, IL: Tyndale House.

Ignatius of Loyola. 1997. *The Spiritual Exercises of St. Ignatius.* Translated by Pierre Wolff. Garden City, NY: Image.

Keating, Thomas. 1995. *Open Mind, Open Heart: The Contemplative Dimension of the Gospel.* New York: Continuum Press.

Kelley, Thomas. 1996. *A Testament of Devotion.* San Francisco: HarperSanFrancisco.

Kelsey, Morton. 1997. *The Other Side of Silence.* New York: Paulist Press.

Keyes, Ken. 1990. *The Handbook to Higher Consciousness.* Emeryville, CA: Publishers Group West.

Kosinski, Jerzy. 1995. *The Painted Bird.* New York: Grove/Atlantic.

Lawrence, Brother. 1977. *Practice of the Presence of God.* Garden City, New York: Image.

Lindberg, Anne Morrow. 1991. *Gift From the Sea*. New York: Pantheon.

May, Gerald. 1991. *Addiction and Grace*. San Francisco: HarperSanFrancisco.

_____. 1991. *The Awakened Heart*. New York: Harper Collins.

McFague, Sallie. 1987. *Models of God: Theology for an Ecological Nuclear Age*. Minneapolis: Fortress Press.

Merton, Thomas. 1987. *Thoughts in Solitude*. New York: Farrar, Straus and Giroux.

Missine, Leo E. 1990. *Reflections on Aging: A Spiritual Guide*. Liquori, MO: Liquori Press.

Oliver, Mary Anne McPherson. 1994. *Conjugal Spirituality: The Primacy of Mutual Love in Christian Tradition*. Kansas City, MO: Sheed and Ward.

Newman, John Henry. 1940. "Lead Kindly Light", Hymn #430 in *The Hymnal of the Protestant Episcopal Church in the United States of America*. New York: Church Hymnal Corp.

Peck, M. Scott. 1997. *The Road Less Traveled*. New York: Touchstone.

Pennington, M. Basil. 1987. *Centering Prayer*. Garden City, NY: Image.

_____. 1998. *Lectio Divina: Renewing the Ancient Practice of Praying the Scriptures*. New York: Crossroad Publications.

Phillips, John B. 1997. *Your God is Too Small*. New York: Macmillan.

References

Progoff, Ira. 1992. *At a Journal Workshop.* New York: Tarcher.

Raines, Robert. 1997. *A Time to Live: Seven Tasks of Creative Aging.* New York: Dutton.

Rupp, Joyce. 1988. *Praying Our Goodbyes.* Notre Dame, IN: University of Notre Dame Press.

St. Teresa of Avila. 1972. *Interior Castle.* Garden City, NY: Image.

Schaef, Ann Wilson. 1990. *Meditations for Women Who Do Too Much.* San Francisco: HarperSanFrancisco.

Shalomi, Zalman Schacter and Ronald S. Miller. 1995. *From Age-ing to Sage-ing.* New York: Warner Books.

Tiellard de Chardin, Pierre. 1989. *The Divine Milieu.* New York: Harper Collins.

Thibault, Jane. 1993. *A Deepening Love Affair: The Gift of God in Later Life.* Nashville: Upper Room Books.

Thompson, Francis. 1986. *The Hound of Heaven.* New York: Morehouse Press.

Thompson, Marjorie. 1995. *Soul Feast: An Invitation to the Christian Spiritual Life.* Louisville, KY: Westminster John Knox Press.

Vest, Norvene. 1990. *Preferring Christ: A Devotional Commentary and Workbook on the Rule of Saint Benedict.* Trabuco Canyon, CA: Source Books.

Walker, Alice. 1998. *The Color Purple.* New York: Washington Square Press.

Wiederkehr, Macrina. 1988. *A Tree Full of Angels: Seeing the Holy in the Ordinary.* San Francisco: Harper Collins.

Wise, Lois. 1994. *Women Make the Best Friends.* New York: Simon and Schuster.

Yeats, William Butler. 1996. "Sailing to Byzantium." In *The Complete Poems of W. B. Yeats.* Edited by Richard J. Finneran. New York: Scribner.

Yungblut, John. 1994. *The Gentle Art of Spiritual Guidance.* Rockport, MA: Element.

Retreat and Workshop Topics

Spirituality:

- Introduction to Prayer
- Tools for the Spiritual Journey:
- Letting Go and Moving On: Moving Through Life's Transitions
- Waiting: A Gift of God to a Busy World
- Introduction to Spiritual Direction
- The Prayer Journal
- Crisis as a Vehicle for Growth

Myers-Briggs Type Indicator:

- Understanding Myself
- Type and the Family
- Type and the Prayer Journey

Aging:

- Aging as a Spiritual Pilgrimage
- Caring for the Caregiver
- The Sandwich Generation
- Life Review: Living forward, Looking Back
- Older Women's Issues
- Spiritual Mentoring as a Late Life Ministry
- Spirituality and Sexuality in the Second Half of Life

Lynn also works in areas of Evangelism and Congregational Concerns.

For additional information and for other topics she may be reached at lotus.spirit@comcast.net p48- , bottom of page – Paul quote

God works... who <u>love</u> <u>the</u> <u>lord</u>" vs

Universe benefiting everyone w/o
qualifier ??